Glass-Steagall and the 2008 Global Financial Crisis

Copyright © 2022 James Michael Branam

All rights reserved. No part of this publication may be reproduced, distributed, or transmitted in any form or by any means, including photocopying, recording, or other electronic or mechanical methods, without the prior written permission of the publisher, except in the case of brief quotations embodied in critical reviews and certain other noncommercial uses permitted by copyright law.

ISBN: 9798371706713 (Paperback)
ISBN: 9798371735720 (Hardcover)

First printing edition 2022

Glass-Steagall
and the
2008 Global Financial Crisis

By James Branam

Table of Contents

INTRODUCTION 9
1. PREVENTING A CRISIS 19
   1.1 The Glass-Steagall Act 23
   1.2 Separation 27
   1.3 Securities and Financial Derivatives 31
   1.4 Federal Deposit Insurance 35
   1.5 Transfer of Securities and Derivatives 37
   1.6 The Act 1933-1988 39
2. DEREGULATION 43
   2.1 A History of Presidential Involvement 49
   2.2 A Crisis Is Born 57
3. A FULL-BLOWN CRISIS 61
4. THE TOOLS OF A CRISIS 75
   4.1 Subprime Mortgages 77
   4.2 Credit Default Swaps 79
   4.3 Faulty Ratings 83
5. THE FAILURE OF GIANTS 87
   5.1 The Auto Industry Crisis 93
   5.2 Failure of the Fed 99

6. THE BAILOUTS 101
6.1 Saving the Banks 103
6.2 Rescuing the Automakers 105
6.3 Glass-Steagall and Bailouts 109
7. CONCLUSION 111
LIST OF GRAPHS AND TABLES 125
Graphs 125
Tables 125
BIBLIOGRAPHY 127
REFERENCES 129
ACKNOWLEDGEMENTS 133
PUBLICATIONS BY JAMES BRANAM 135
AUTHOR BIOGRAPHY 137

INTRODUCTION

In English, there is well-known saying that when something important is going on, silence is a lie. No truer words could have been spoken and no more accurate assessment could have been made, especially of the financial crisis of 2008. One of the biggest financial crises to befall the world would eventually wreak havoc, decimate assets, and destroy futures without preference as to class, race, gender, or nationality. Warning signs were completely ignored, data purposely skewed, and individuals taken advantage of, all in the name of financial gains and profits. In hindsight, those individuals and institutions who could have issued warnings did nothing of the sort; they simply remained silent. Therefore, by doing nothing, they might have been equally guilty as those who acted. "How could anyone deny something had gone badly awry?" (Mirowski, 2014, p. 30). Using a theoretical approach, this thesis will attempt to show that, if the proper authorities had not been silent, and if certain laws and regulations had been left in place, the crisis could have been avoided, at least partially.

Historians will argue that financial crises are not a new phenomenon; they have occurred since the invention of money. Those with no money have always sought to acquire it; others
with too much money have needed to invest it lest it be stolen, spent, or lost. Should one belong to the latter group,

investing money usually meant depending on another credible person or institution to look after it, with or without a financial stake. It is often said that the best test of character is to look after the property of another, and in the past, it was usually quite difficult to find an individual or institution worthy of trust.

Historically, a lot of attention has been paid to the phenomenon that is called money. Moreover, when pondered, one soon begins to realize that the coins and banknotes that line the pockets and wallets of the world's inhabitants are, in reality "nothing more than a political creation, a promise to pay between two or more parties, enforced, to a greater or lesser degree by the power of a state" (Engdahl, 2010, p. 2). Furthermore, when looking at money from this angle, it immediately loses some of its mystique, and one is left wondering what the fuss is all about. Is money even worth all the trouble?

The fuss over money is more precisely about its profitability. In most western societies, the act of possessing money is not nearly enough; the goal is to use it to acquire even more money. Therefore, it can be stated that the first financial crises were borne out of a quest to secure great amounts of money, even if this meant taking unfair advantage of the poor, underprivileged, and uneducated. In brief, these cruel acts, inspired by the desire for more and performed throughout time, have nearly always set the stage for subsequent crises in every historical era and in nearly every country in the world. No nation has remained unscathed from the consequences of such actions. The 2008 crisis is no exception.

The United States of America, a global financial power since the early twentieth century, has not remained immune to financial crises. In fact, the financial crises of the U.S. can be traced back to the eighteenth century when coins and furs were used as currency. By the time the United States of America had gained complete independence from Great Britain in 1781 (when the Revolutionary War ended), paper money had already taken hold in the colonies, negating the previous need to barter with furs. Soon, paper money was being used everywhere to make financial transactions for all types of goods. It was also being invested in order to make more money. Where there was money, crisis soon followed.

The Industrial Revolution of the nineteenth century saw even more of the same, but to a much greater extent. In nearly every state of the new nation, millionaires were made and un-made. However, the ones who had eventually risen to great financial heights, amassing their fortunes using paper money, were also the first to fall. Scandals became rampant. Paper money, being easy to produce, was being printed by states and, in some cases, even communities. While this increased the options for investment, it also created the potential for enormous risk, and "risks always come back to bite someone" (Warren, 2017, p. 82). Those investors who had made the right decisions as to which currency to invest in soon found themselves in very good condition, indeed. However, the question was not if one had enough, but rather if one had it all.

The twentieth century started with a bang – at least financially. Modern tax laws hadn't yet been enacted, and the situation over time essentially put the fate of the young American nation in the hands of a few very rich individuals. One of these individuals was J.P. Morgan, a wealthy American financier who once said that if you have to ask how much it costs, you can't afford it.

J.P. Morgan, often called the father of modern banking and investment, is also credited with helping to put in place the foundations of the modern financial crisis in 1907 by issuing

> a rumor that a competing unnamed large bank was about to fail. It was a false charge, but customers nonetheless raced to their banks to withdraw their money. As they pulled out their funds, the banks lost their deposits and were forced to call in their loans (Chossudovsky and Marshall, 2010, p. 61-62).

However, a new financial institution was created as well. "In 1907, J.P. Morgan's irresponsible actions caused panic that resulted in a crash that prompted the creation of the Federal Reserve, a private banking cartel with the veneer of an independent government organization" (Chossudovsky and Marshall, 2010, p. 62). This is the same Federal Reserve that would play a huge role in the

Great Depression of the 1930s and remain mostly inactive during the Great Recession of 2008.

Normally, the creation of an independent regulatory organization to oversee the financial sector would have been viewed as a positive development, but things did not exactly progress as the creators of 'The Fed'[1] had envisioned. In fact, The Fed "doubled America's money supply within five years, and in 1920, it called in a mass percentage of [its] loans. Over five thousand banks collapsed overnight" (*ibid.*, p. 62), with citizens rushing the banks and demanding the prompt return of their savings. Moreover, this dire situation occurred even despite the financial gains that had been previously gained owing to the reluctance of the U.S. government to enter World War I and the profits from supplying the Triple Entente[2] with military equipment and arms. (It has also been reported by historians that the U.S. also supplied countries belonging to the Central Powers[3].)

When the U.S. did finally enter the war in 1917, it was nearly over[4]. Although great numbers of troops were sent abroad to participate in the war, very few American causalities were suffered, at least when compared to other

---

[1] The Federal Reserve Bank is often shortened to the abbreviation 'The Fed'.
[2] The Triple Entente consisted primarily of the United Kingdom, France, and Russia, and was created to prevent Germany and Austria-Hungary from conquering more of continental Europe.
[3] The Central Powers consisted primarily of Germany, Austria-Hungary, Bulgaria, and the Ottoman Empire.
[4] The U.S. entered the war in April 1917. World War I ended in November 2018.

major wars of the twentieth century. It can be argued that all wars are crises in themselves, and the real financial crisis began when thousands of soldiers began returning to the U.S after their brief stint in the war.

The U.S. labor market had changed somewhat while they were away, with thousands of women joining the workforce, picking up where needed. The economy was at that time in no state to adequately integrate the returning soldiers. These repatriated soldiers needed places to live and, with the wartime pay they had received during the war, they needed a place to spend and invest their money. Banks started springing up everywhere, and there were very few regulations in place to govern them. Thus, the system was ripe for a financial catastrophe. It did not have to wait long. After a few years of rampant consumerism known as the 'Roaring Twenties,'[5] the ensuing 1920 crisis hit the market where it mattered most: the banks. Banks crashed everywhere, depositors lost their hard-earned assets, and utter chaos reigned in the financial sector. Things were very bad, but they were about to get much worse.

The real financial catastrophe, at least the one that comes to mind when considering the early twentieth century, came in the form of the Great Depression. As taught in most American schools, the crisis began with the 1929 stock market crash[6]. 'Black Friday,' as the day the

---

[5] The "Roaring Twenties" refers to the years of 1920-1929.
[6] Signs of an impending financial crisis were already evident, but they were ignored by most financial experts.

stock market crashed has been named, would usher in hard times for most Americans, but it was not until after "the United States [had] experienced a stock market boom, which was a result of the commercial banks providing funds for the purchase of stock and took the latter as collateral, creating a massive wave of underwriting and purchasing of securities. The stock market speculation that followed was a result of the banks" (Chossudovsky and Marshall, 2010, p. 314).

Graph 1: Common Stock Prices, 1920-1935

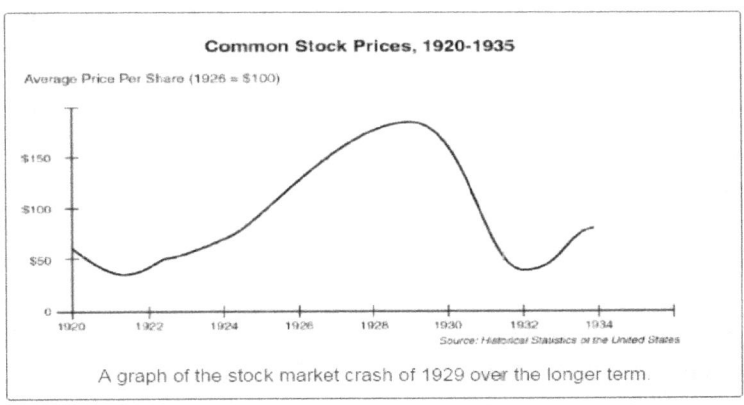

A graph of the stock market crash of 1929 over the longer term.

Source: The Great Recession Blog, online, accessed 2017-10-09.

The United States was brought to its knees by this event. It "eventually led to a worldwide financial depression. It was particularly acute in the United States, where unemployment rose to 25 percent, and nearly one in five homeowners faced foreclosures" (Ritholtz, 2009, p. 24). Most of the population of the U.S. was devastated. Thousands of banks failed, millions of jobs were lost, and in October 1929, the stock market took a dangerous nosedive, with investors losing more than $14 billion. Around the nation, people of all ages, all races, and nearly all classes waited in lines for food; many migrated to parts of the country that were much less affected, like the southwest; and nearly every family in the United States was affected, to various degrees.

By the end of the Great Depression, suffering had reached all areas of society except for the upper class. The U.S. government tried to create real solutions to help the average citizen overcome the crisis. To help ease the burden, thousands of savings and loan banks were "established as separately regulated banks during the depression years to provide a secure source of long-term mortgage credit to family home buyers" (Engdahl, 2010, p. 25). For most people, this help came too late and would not go far enough. The crisis would have to be overcome individually through hard work, perseverance, and a lot of luck.

As a historical note, many of these [savings and loan banks) would fail before the Great Depression ended as "banks failed in waves from 1930 through 1933" (Carpenter et al., 2016, p. 3, online, accessed 2017-01-06). In essence, "the overall financial system at that time was in bankruptcy" (Ogden, 2015, p. 16).

Most financial experts consider the Great Depression a crisis that could have been avoided, if not completely then at least somewhat. "Most economists, to the extent that they think about the subject at all, regard the Great Depression of the 1930s as a gratuitous, unnecessary tragedy" (Krugman, 2009, p. 3). However, at that time the situation in the United States was indeed ripe for financial change. It was time to protect citizens from future crises, and most people accepted government involvement as the only manner in which this could be accomplished. Government regulations would provide the type of financial security that was needed for its citizens to thrive. "The result was the creation of a system with many more safeguards" (*ibid.*, p. 157). Thus, the Glass-Steagall Act was born. "This [act] then opened the way for the recovery from the Great Depression" (Ogden, 2015, p. 17). Financial regulation would follow.

The Glass-Steagall Act was enacted by the U.S. congress in 1933. The years following the passing of the act by the U.S. Congress were among the most financially sound in the short history of the United States. The country and its citizens prospered, and the nation soon found itself at the top of the global financial ladder, setting examples for others to emulate for more than sixty-five years. However, this would soon start to change over time, culminating in another great financial crisis.

The Great Recession of 2008 brought to an end the remaining safeguards that had been put in place after the

Great Depression. It is noteworthy that the crisis could have been prevented had the provisions of the Glass-Steagall Act that had been created following the Great Depression been left in place. However, the search for more profits would once again prevail. Free from the limitations of Glass-Steagall, banks were left to regulate themselves. These banks along with other financial institutions merged and grew into unforeseen giants, and "when a handful of giants dominate, markets don't work very well" (Warren, 2017, p. 88). Thus, the actions of the few would once again have an enormous impact on the many. In brief, when governments "let the big corporations do whatever they want. What could possibly go wrong?" (*ibid.*, p. 80).

Everything went wrong. Unknowing citizens who had no idea that they would be participants in one of the greatest scams in modern history, were robbed of their savings, banks and corporations failed, and the bottom soon fell out of the financial sector. Financial malpractice, fiscal recklessness, and foolish speculations were eventually punished by the market" (Ritholtz, 2009, p. 4), but it was completely unnecessary and would have been mostly prevented by Glass-Steagall. However, such was the Great Recession of 2008, the largest preventable global financial crisis to ever occur.

1. PREVENTING A CRISIS

Although investments made by financial institutions and individuals were not the sole cause of the Great Depression, they did play a major part in its occurrence. After the Great Depression in the early part of the twentieth century, the U.S. government realized that something could be done to lessen the impact of financial stability for future generations. After years of long deliberation and exemplary collaboration between both major political parties, the Glass-Steagall Act was created and subsequently enacted by the U.S. Congress. This act, "passed amid the national bank panic in the first days of Roosevelt's administration, dealt a devastating blow to the once almighty House of Morgan, a blow from which it never fully recovered" (Engdahl, 2010, p. 122). Rightly, J.P. Morgan, the man whose reckless acts had created the first financial crisis of the twentieth century in 1907 would inspire the law that would prohibit such crises in the future.

Named after congressional sponsors Carter Glass and Henry Steagall, the act would go a long way in helping to prevent another financial crisis. Its goal was to limit investment by banks by separating commercial banking from investment banking and insurance. In other words, the act was created to prevent banks from the prior practice of

> *investing their own assets in securities, with consequent risk to commercial and savings depositories in the event of a stock crash. Unsound loans were made by banks in order to artificially prop up the price of select securities or the financial position of companies in which a bank had invested its own assets. A bank's financial interest in the ownership, pricing, or distribution of securities inevitably tempted bank officials to press their banking customers into investing securities which the bank itself was under pressure to sell. It was a colossal conflict of interest and invitation to fraud and abuse* (Engdahl, 2010, p. 311).

Moreover, it made perfect sense to lawmakers to regulate such matters as financial investment as the American people were neither in the position, nor had they the power to do so themselves. The Glass-Steagall Act would come into play whenever "a commercial bank goes beyond the business of acting as fiduciary or managing agent and enters the investment banking business either directly or by establishing an affiliate to hold and sell particular investments" (Engdahl, 2010, p. 312). The U.S. government would essentially be required to play the part of the financial watchdog for the average citizen and to ensure the total transparency of the banking and financial industry.

Although it was quite difficult to enforce the new law in the years following its enactment, "the new system protected the economy from financial crises" (Krugman, 2009, p. 157). Moreover, the act would eventually "break up the bank holding companies with their inherent conflicts of interest that had led tens of millions into joblessness and home foreclosures in the 1930s depression" (Engdahl, 2010, p. 316). The financial sector was initially in shock by the measures taken by the U.S. government, but the American public could see that Congress was actively taking steps in trying to avoid such financial disasters in the future. The future would be regulated by the Glass-Steagall Act, "a pillar of President Roosevelt's New Deal, which was put in place in response to the climate of corruption, financial manipulation and insider trading that resulted in more than 5,000 bank failures in the years following the 1929 Wall Street crash" (Chossudovsky and Marshall, 2010, p. 35).

1.1 The Glass-Steagall Act

The Glass-Steagall Act was not a law in itself, but rather a subset of the provisions set out by the Banking Act of 1933. However, many today refer to the Banking Act of 1933 as the Glass-Steagall Act. The act's provisions were created in order to "provide for the safer and more effective use of the assets of banks, to regulate interbank control, and to prevent the undue diversion of funds into speculative operations, and for other purposes" (Carpenter et al., 2016, p. 5, online, accessed 2017-01-06). It forced players in the financial industry to take sides, as "bankers had to make a choice between low-risk, boring banking and high risk, Wall Street-style investing. One or the other – but not both" (Warren, 2017, p. 69). The Glass-Steagall Act's language was clear and left little to the imagination (and few legal loopholes), and it created a foundation for financial regulation. Moreover, "the new system protected the economy from financial crises" (Krugman, 2009, p. 157) for years to come.

Banks and other financial institutions were certainly no fans of the new legislation. In fact, "business leaders in the 1930s strongly objected to the government oversight and regulation that came with taxpayer largesse" (Ritholtz, 2009, p. 25). However, by separating the two branches, losses could be minimalized and conflicts of interest could be avoided. Moreover, by creating a barrier between these two types of institutions, the act essentially limited the amount and type of financial damage that could have been inflicted on the American population. In hindsight, it took a great catastrophe to create the need for the Glass-Steagall Act, and this exactly how the act came to be. "The insured commercial banks under Glass-Steagall [could] potentially then invest, to contribute to a recovery of growth and productive employment" (Ogden, 2015, p. 17), and this is exactly what the nation needed. Thus, "the greatest recovery action in the recent history of the United States" (*ibid.*, p. 17) had begun.

Huge changes to any industry can be painful and very difficult to carry out. Resistance is common, and
in some cases, due to lack of foresight and patience, institutions can be found protesting against their own interests.

However, in the years that followed the creation of Glass-Steagall, financial institutions slowly began to realize that the Glass-Steagall Act did not signify the end of banking, but rather a new beginning, one filled with security and growth. In fact, "bank regulation steadied the financial system. It was a good deal for the banks, a good deal for the depositors, and a good deal for the U.S. economy" (Warren, 2017, p. 69). The provisions set in place by Glass-Steagall helped to provide financial stability during the ensuing Great Depression and on through World War II. It underlined the miraculous financial growth of the U.S. economy during the post-war years and throughout the 1950s. However, by the turbulent 1960s, the act had fallen subject to various interpretations, by the banks themselves and by other institutions. Despite these interpretations and unforeseen challenges, the Glass-Stegall Act primarily did set out to do what it was designed to do: rein in fraud by limiting the activities of banks and financial institutions.

1.2 Separation

The Glass-Steagall act was a complex piece of legislation. The act included four regulatory components. The first of these components required commercial banks, investment banks, broker-dealers, and insurance companies to be separated from one another. Even management or ownership could not be shared among them. This presented a huge problem for some institutions as their banking and investment activities were often intertwined. However, they were forced to separate the two branches to comply with the provisions of the law. Investing in "securities was limited so that banks could no longer participate in speculative securities operations" (Carpenter et al., 2016, online, accessed 2017-01-06). This was not a new restriction, and had been the case for the better part of the ten years running up to the act's enacting. The Banking Act of 1933 is very clear in stating that the

> dealing in investment securities by the association shall be limited to purchasing and selling such securities without recourse, solely upon the order, and for the account of, customers, and in no case for its own account, and the association shall not underwrite any issue of securities (ibid., p. 5, online, accessed 2017-01-06).

This restriction was designed with the consumer in mind, in that the limitations in question were not in the interest of anyone except the investing institution or bank. "One problem that Glass-Steagall was designed to address was that, prior to 1929, banks had been investing their own assets in securities, with consequent risk to commercial and savings depositories in the event of a stock crash" (Engdahl, 2010, p. 311). Securities were broken down into bank-eligible and bank-ineligible securities. Sometimes "a bank's financial interest in the ownership, pricing, or distribution of securities inevitably tempted bank officials to press their banking customers into investing in securities which the bank itself was under pressure to sell" (Engdahl, 2009, p. 311). These guidelines were designed to tighten the limitations on investment banking and limit the potential for fraud. The Glass-Steagall Act's provisions also prohibited banks from

> the association of any shares of stock of any corporation. The limitations and restrictions herein contained as to dealing in, underwriting and purchasing for its own account, investment securities shall not apply to obligations of the United States, or to general obligations of any State or of any political subdivision thereof, or obligations issued under authority of the Federal Farm Loan Act, as amended, or issued by the Federal Home Loan Banks or the Home Owners Loan Corporation (Carpenter et al., 2016, p. 6, online, accessed 2017-01-06)

This was an indirect limitation on banks, covering potentially more funds that could be accessed by financial institutions. This essentially prohibited member banks of the Federal Reserve system from doing business with companies that do the majority of their business in securities activities (Carpenter et al., 2016, online, accessed 2017-01-06).

1.3 Securities and Financial Derivatives

The next section of the Glass-Steagall Act defines and addresses investment in securities that had little to do with actual banking and financial derivatives. While altogether banning investment in derivatives, some securities investment was allowed. However, the act "makes it illegal for a firm to engage in both deposit taking and investment banking, except the 'bank-eligible securities' allowed under Section 16" (Carpenter et al., 2016, online, accessed 2017-01-06). More specifically,

> for any person, firm, corporation, association, business trust, or other similar organization, engaged in the business of issuing, underwriting, selling, or distributing, at wholesale or retail, or through syndicate participation, stocks, bonds, debentures, notes, or other securities, to engage at the same time to any extent whatever in the business of receiving deposits subject to check or to repayment upon presentation of a passbook, certificate of deposit, or other evidence of debt, or upon request of the depositor (Carpenter et al., 2016, p. 6, online, accessed 2017-01-06).

When most people refer to the Glass-Steagall provision, they have this part of the Banking Act in mind. It is also the section with the least amount of ambiguity and it leaves nothing to the imagination of the individual or institution. However, to cover all bases, the act addresses even the employees of financial institutions. In order to provide provisions that cover the entirety of the financial sector, and to include the indirect investment of customer funds, the final section of the Glass-Steagall Act from the Banking Act of 1933 clearly states that

> no officer or director of any member bank shall be an officer, director, or manager of any corporation, partnership, or unincorporated association engaged primarily in the business of purchasing, selling, or negotiating securities, and no member bank shall perform the functions of a correspondent for any member bank or hold on deposit any funds on behalf of any member bank, unless in any such case there is a permit therefor issued by the Federal Reserve Board; and the Board is authorized to issue such permit if in its judgment it is not incompatible with the public interest, and to revoke any such permit whenever it finds after reasonable notice and opportunity to be heard, that the public interest requires such revocation (Carpenter et al., 2016, p. 7, online, accessed 2017-01-06).

Incidentally, it was this section that was violated with the greatest frequency throughout the years that followed and until early into the next century. It was also proven the most difficult to prosecute in U.S. courts, and in many cases, perpetrators of such crimes were acquitted and very rarely had to serve time when they were indeed found to be guilty.

1.4 Federal Deposit Insurance

The third provision of the Glass-Steagall Act was the creation of the Federal Deposit Insurance Corporation. Created to support banks and their depositors, the F.D.I.C., as it is commonly known, has been a study fixture of the financial sector even until today. The F.D.I.C.'s purpose is to insure deposits against bank failure. Deposits of up to $250,000 are insured (in some cases more), and the F.D.I.C. covers nearly every type of banking transaction. However, investment activity such as stocks, bonds, and mutual funds are not insured, as this could violate the provisions of the Glass-Steagall Act that address separation of commercial banking and investment. Today, when shopping for banks, most American consumers check to see whether the bank being considered is insured by the F.D.I.C. This can be as easy as looking at the front door of the bank, where an F.D.I.C. is usually displayed.

1.5 Transfer of Securities and Derivatives

The fourth component of the Glass-Steagall Act addresses risky securities and derivatives. According to the act, securities and derivatives that are deemed as risky cannot be transferred within a holding company to a commercial bank. By transferring these risky investments to banks, taxpayer funds would eventually be responsible for the coverage, should they fail. This provision of the act was put in place to close loopholes that might arise from the other three provisions. However, despite this provision's inclusion in the Glass-Steagall Act, it has been violated more often than one would expect, and to some degree of success. Even when caught, banks often rely on lawyers to find even more loopholes allowing the bank to continue engaging in the prohibited activity.

1.6 The Act 1933-1988

The Glass-Steagall Act is one of the most important pieces of legislation to be enacted by the U.S. Congress in the twentieth century. Its creation helped to shape the manner in which banks and other financial institutions conducted themselves for many years to come. "Banks that offered investment banking services and mutual funds were subject to conflicts of interest and other abuses, thereby harming their customers, including borrowers, depositors, and correspondent banks. The Glass-Steagall Act of 1933 was specifically intended to prevent this" (Engdahl, 2010, p. 311) activity. The U.S. government knew that some would protest the new legislation, which did indeed happen. In particular, there was a great deal of protest in the years before World War II, but this protest was later dampened owing to the involvement of the U.S. in the war. Protests occurred even despite the law's success and the overall calm it had brought to the financial sector. "Once the new financial regulations were in place, from the mid-1930s forward, America experienced decade after decade of economic peace" (Warren, 2017, p. 75). Sadly, the end of the war brought more protests, but to a much lesser extent. "After World War II, the United States entered a long period of economic expansion" (Ritholtz, 2009, p. 11). The U.S. population was slowly getting used to the act, and financial institutions, which had started to experience stability and even growth, considered it prudent to adhere to its provisions.

The Glass-Steagall Act, while effective, was certainly not perfect legislation. Despite efforts to close them, some minor loopholes and workarounds remained, and even today economists speak about the act's shortcomings. It is a well-known fact that
> while the Glass-Steagall Act generally prohibited depository banks from competing in securities markets as broker-dealers and underwriters, the only activities-based restriction on securities firms and their employees contained in the Glass-Steagall Act and the complementary securities laws relevant to this discussion was the prohibition on accepting deposits. These laws did not prohibit securities market professionals from using securities markets to fund private debt in competition with, or even in conjunction with, commercial banks (Carpenter et al., 2016, p. 7, online, accessed 2017-01-06).

Some of these exemptions would be utilized for many years by financial institutions in nearly every state. However, the law was still strong enough to prevent the majority of fraudulent investments from occurring. In fact, "in the short term, the Glass-Steagall Act, in combination with complementary securities laws, erected a rigid wall separating commercial banks and securities firms" (Carpenter et al., 2016, p. 7, online, accessed 2017-01-06). The real question was how much pressure the wall could withstand. How would the Glass-Steagall Act stand the test of time?

The Glass-Steagall Act proved to be sturdier than anyone had expected. Stability ensued in the financial sector. However, as it is, good things usually come to an end. "Over the course of the nearly 70-year-long Glass-Steagall era, the separation of traditional commercial banking and securities activities gradually eroded. This erosion was the result of a confluence of matters, including market changes, statutory changes, and regulatory and judicial interpretations" (*ibid.*, p. 8). By the end of the 1990's, and after much deregulation of various types of investment, it was President Bill Clinton, under pressure from Congress, who would deal the death blow to the act.

2. DEREGULATION

Despite the Glass-Steagall Act's undeniable initial success, by 1990 opponents from across the political spectrum had begun calling for its repeal. These opponents argued that the act stymied growth and negatively impacted investment for both the public and the banks on which the act focused. With investment limited, in editorial cartoons, the Glass-Steagall Act was often depicted as a ball and chain attached to the ankle of the Statue of Liberty. Raghuram Rajan, an open-minded economist from Chicago wrote that "the Glass-Steagall Act had constituted unnecessary regulation back in the 1930s, because commingling of investment and commercial banking had not ratcheted up riskiness of the entire system" (In Mirowski, 2014, p. 180). Other economists and financial experts along with banks and other financial institutions began lobbying the U.S. government to find a way to replace or terminate the legislation. Year by year, more U.S. representatives and senators came out against the act, calling for its immediate deactivation. This pressure eventually led President William Clinton (with bipartisan support) to repeal the act in 1999 and replace it with the Gramm-Leach-Bliley Act[7]. "Adopted by the U.S. Congress in the wake of lengthy negotiations" (Chossudovsky and Marshall, 2010, p. 35), this new act reversed decades of

---

[7] The Gramm-Leach-Bliley Act is often referred to as the Financial Services Modernization Act of 1999.

controls set in place by the Glass-Steagall Act, and basically provided free reign to banks and financial institutions as to how they decided to invest their own and their customers' assets. Essentially,

> congress had passed Glass-Steagall in the first place precisely in order to break up the bank holding companies with their inherent conflicts of interest that had led tens of millions of Americans into joblessness and home foreclosures in the 1930s depression. In 1999, this protection vanished (Engdahl, 2010, p. 316).

The act also "reversed the rules that prohibited bank holding companies from owning other financial firms" (Ritholtz, 2009, p. 135). And subsequently, "this allowed insurers, banks, and brokerage firms to merge into giant financial centers" (*ibid.*, p. 135).

Deregulation was not an easy victory for opponents of the Glass-Steagall Act. "The issues provoked a hard fight in Congress that lasted until the final repeal of Glass-Steagall. The Gramm-Leach-Bliley Act was signed into law by President Clinton in 1999" (Engdahl, 2010, p. 315). Supporters of President Clinton were thrilled by the creation of the Gramm-Leach-Bliley Act, and ultimately give him credit for the financial gains that subsequently followed. They
argued that "just before [Clinton] left office, he dumped Glass-Steagall, and that caused the great Wall Street boom" (Speed, 2015, p. 60). Others were less accepting of

the President and congress enacting Gramm-Leach-Bliley, stating that "cancellation of Glass-Steagall was actually a treason against the United States, in fact. It might not be recognized as such, but to anyone who is looking at it from an economic or scientific standpoint, that was a crime against the United States" (*ibid.*, p. 60).

It is not just the enactment of Gramm-Leach-Bliley that the Clinton administration is best remembered for. "Under President Bill Clinton, several key legislative proposals were passed that reduced oversight and supervision" (Ritholtz, 2009, p. 135), and after Glass-Steagall was repealed, the U.S. economy continued to grow, but at a much faster rate. Silicon Valley grew even faster (eventually leading to the dotcom bubble in 2000-1)[8]. Moreover, "the repeal of the Glass-Steagall Act had created an environment which favored an unprecedented concentration of global financial power" (Chossudovsky and Marshall, 2010, p. 39).

This time in history is often called the "Era of Big Banks." Banks, financial institutions, and Savings and Loans banks merged and formed super-banks; financial institutions bought other financial institutions; and "the new law had opened the doors of the S&Ls to wholesale financial abuses and wild speculative risks as never before" (Engdahl, 2010, p. 298). The financial sector, after enjoying decades of calm and stability found itself in the middle of a power play for more wealth and bigger market

---

[8] The dotcom bubble is said to have built up in 1997-9, and burst in 2000-1.

shares. It became a winner-take-all situation in which the potential for one to become very rich was great, but where the fall would be devastating should one not succeed.

In 1999, the first of several major falls occurred in the form of the dotcom bubble. By 1999, the dotcom bubble was in full swing with literally thousands of new corporations cashing in on the success of internet-based applications and services. "What had emerged after the 1999 repeal of Glass-Steagall was an awesome transformation of American credit markets into what would soon become the world's greatest unregulated private money-creating machine" (*ibid.*, p. 324). Everyone was trying to get a piece of the pie, but in reality, everyone was left hungry to pick up the financial crumbs.

Graph 2: NASDAQ Composite

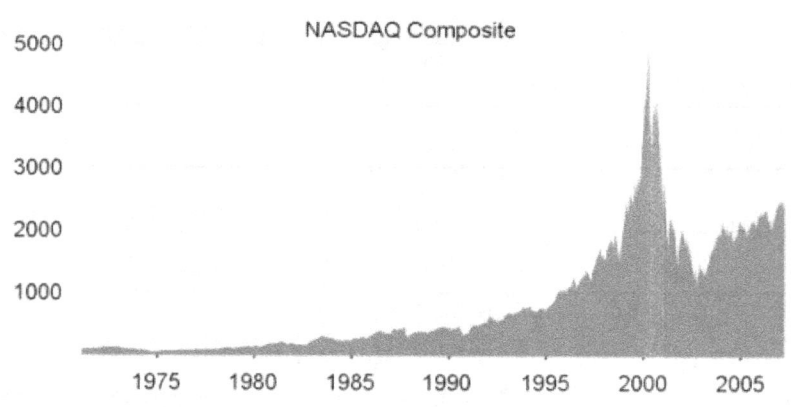

Source: The JohnnyStartup Blog, online, accessed 2017-11-10.

The years following the dotcom bubble were tumultuous at best. Americans became more cautious with their investments lest another bubble appear and rob them of their financial investments. After the terrorist attacks of September 11, 2001, the U.S. was at war in Afghanistan and Iraq, and the last thing needed by the American people was another bubble. Investments became more conservative, and investors started to concentrate more on real estate and similar types of investment. However, despite this demonstrated caution, the markets did rebound, and not long after the dotcom bubble, stability and investor confidence had returned, leading again to riskier investments. So much confidence had returned that the Dow Jones index began reaching new highs, and investors began ignoring the troubling signs around them that a new crisis was fast approaching. This crisis would rip apart the foundations of investor confidence, leaving virtually nothing in its wake. The Great Recession of 2008 would change the way the financial world operated in the future.

2.1 A History of Presidential Involvement

The Gramm-Leach Bliley Act was by no means the beginning or even the end of financial deregulation. "The history of deregulation goes back to the beginnings of the Reagan administration" (Chossudovsky and Marshall, 2010, p. 25-26), and even before that, to the collapse of Breton Woods. Essentially a "new global financial environment... unfolded in several stages since the collapse of the Breton Woods system of fixed exchange rate in 1971" (*ibid.*, p. 25). For years, since the collapse of Breton Woods, the U.S. Republican Party has been pushing for more and more financial deregulation, whether it be for investment or lending. Republicans sought to provide banks and other financial institutions with more guarantees that there would be no persecution for the violation of any of Glass-Steagall's four provisions. The result was that banks became more brazen with their activities while pressure to deregulate increased.

The situation was ripe for a U.S. President to act on the limitations of Glass-Steagall. Then, "the debt crisis of the early 1980s broadly coinciding with the Reagan-Thatcher era) had unleashed a wave of corporate mergers, buyouts and bankruptcies" (*ibid.*, p. 25-26). This in turn set the stage for further developments. Big banks became bigger banks; bigger banks became financial behemoths. Investors had become more complacent with their investments. Red flags popped up everywhere, yet they remained unnoticed by the very people they were intended to warn.

It is known throughout both the financial and political spheres that Ronald "Reagan is the intellectual father of the modern radical regulatory movement" (Ritholtz, 2009, p. 134), and he thought that "financial and corporate regulations were the biggest problem faced by Americans." (Warren, 2017, p. 79).

Some thought that the regulations were put in place at a time when they were necessary, while others argued that the U.S. had progressed since that time, and the regulations were no longer necessary.The Republican Party started to speak about deregulation more often, and in a matter of years, the issue had moved to the forefront of the party's agenda. It was placed among other key talking points such as lower taxes and a stronger defense stance. In the eyes of these politicians and the people who voted for them, regulation simply stymied production and growth. So, it is no mystery that "deregulation [had] found an enthusiastic advocate in President Ronald Reagan" (Ritholz, 2009, p. 134), even before he was elected. And it was after taking office that the decision was made to deregulate wherever and whenever possible, regardless of type of industry and scale.

President Ronald Reagan knew that officially, "there had been important alterations in regulatory structures since 1980" (Mirowski, 2014, p. 16), and he knew how to best exploit them. "Deregulation opened a Pandora's Box, unleashing a weird mix of shady off-book operations (SPVs, SIVs) and dodgy, odd-sounding derivatives that were used to amplify leverage and stack debt on tinier and tinier scraps of capital" (Chossudovsky and Marshall, 2010, p. 376). However, deregulation did actually slow in the latter part of the decade, as a timely stock market crash brought down a number of financial institutions. "The 1987 Wall Street crash served to clear the decks so that only the fittest survive" (*ibid.*, p. 29). Essentially, this meant that there were fewer institutions left, but that they would eventually fail harder than ever before.

While the focus is mostly on banks, it is important not to forget the phenomenon of Savings and Loan (S&L) banks. These "banks, established as separately regulated banks during the depression years to provide a secure source of long-term mortgage credit to family home buyers, were deregulated in the early 1980s" (Engdahl, 2010, p. 297). Deregulation of the S&Ls opened a separate box of ills that would immediately infect American investors. S&Ls were very active in issuing mortgages, and mortgages would play a significant role in the financial sector in the near future, a much bigger role than they had ever played before.

Graph 3: Dow Jones (19-Jul-1987 through 19-Jan-1988)

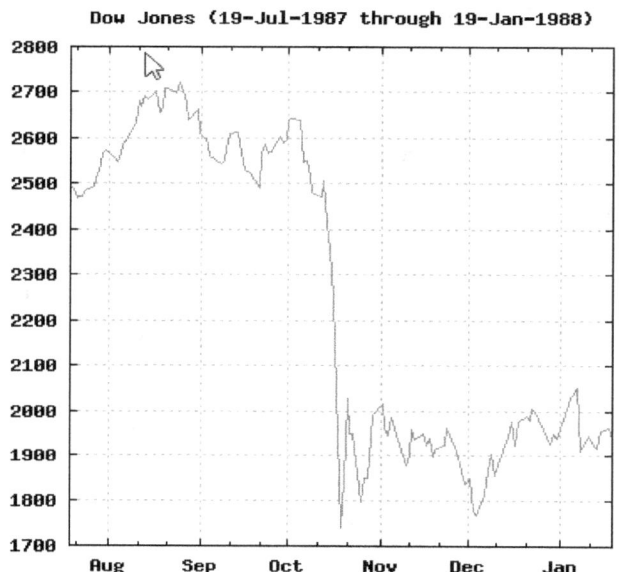

Source: The Market Oracle, online, accessed 2017-11-10.

The first reactions to deregulation were quite favorable. Economists argued that it was time to let banks and corporations regulate themselves, freeing up the government to deal with other, more pressing issues. It turns out that things can go terribly awry when we "let the big corporations do whatever they want. What could possibly go wrong?" (Warren, 2017, p. 80).

By that time, banks had been founded that were already too big to fail, meaning that their failure would have devastating consequences on the U.S. and even global economy. However, "the merger and acquisition boom of the 1990s led to the concurrent consolidation of large corporate entities both in the real economy as well as in banking and financial services" (Chossudovsky and Marshall, 2010, p. 3). In American Society, bigger was better, and this applied to much more than banks. Americans had reached an unsustainable lifestyle and were creating a society more and more reliant on credit. "Advertisers went into overdrive, marketing an ever more luxurious lifestyle, all made available with cheap, easy credit" (*ibid.*, p. 63-64). Credit was everywhere, easy to obtain, and very popular. It was even applied to investment, leading investors to invest far beyond their means. Hedge funds became popular. "One of the most bizarre aspects of the economic crisis of the 1990s was the prominent part played by hedge funds, investment institutions that are able to take temporary control of assets far in excess of their owners' wealth" (Krugman, 2009, p. 120). These hedge funds were difficult to understand for the average American, and even some financial experts were puzzled, forcing them to ask "how big are hedge funds? Nobody really knows because until quite recently nobody thought it was necessary to find out" (*ibid.*, p. 121).

What followed was the riskiest investment error the United States of America had ever experienced. Alan Greenspan and "the Greenspan Fed created an endemic culture of excessive risk taking" (Ritholtz, 2009, p. 58). Deregulation was by then an event in the distant past, and few remembered the original limitations that had been put in place by the Glass-Steagall Act back in 1933. Deregulation had already been accepted as the *status quo*, and "by early 2000, the process of global financial deregulation was in many regards a *fait accompli*" (Chossudovsky and Marshall, 2010, p. 38).

The early years of the 21st are remembered by most as financially prosperous and investor-friendly. Inflation remained bearable, real estate was still considered to be a good investment, and the unemployment rate was acceptable. The only disturbing trend during the decade was the price of oil. "The price of crude oil in mid-2008 had reached 120 dollars a barrel" (*ibid.*, p. 165).

However, with public transportation lacking and even non-existent in most rural areas, Americans had to drive, and they had no choice but to pay more for their fuel. They were essentially being held hostage by OPEC.

Graph 4: The Oil Price Record Since 2002

Source: *The Oil and Gas Journal, online, accessed 2017-11-06.*

It can be seen that from the creation of Glass-Steagall to the Great Recession of the 21st century, "the United States [had] moved from a state of aggressive, post-Depression oversight to one of negligent supervision" (Ritholtz, 2009, p. 135). They had moved from sensible regulation to irresponsible deregulation. It was a free-for-all for financial institutions; nothing was off-limits. "Freed from Glass-Steagall's strictures, money center banks entered onto all manner of underwriting: not just initial public offerings (IPOs) and bond issuance, but structured financial products, including collateralized debt obligations (CDOs) and credit default swaps (CDSs). These derivatives are one of the prime villains in the credit crisis" (*ibid.*, p. 135).

2.2 A Crisis Is Born

In many ways, the financial crisis of 2008 is a direct example of precisely what the Glass-Steagall Act was originally designed to prevent. "With Glass-Steagall gone, the only banks directly monitored by the Federal Reserve were bank holding companies and subsidiary pure lending banks" (Engdahl, 2010, p. 354), and these banks represented only part of financial sector. However, "the repeal of Glass-Steagall wasn't the [sole] cause of the collapse, but it certainly contributed to the crisis being much worse" (Ritholtz, 2009, p. xxvi). Yet, had the Glass-Steagall Act's provisions still been in place at that time, the impact of the crisis would have been significantly less severe, and recovery after the event would have been much easier to attain. The repeal "made the collapse worse, deeper, and more expensive" (Ritholtz, 2009, p. 137).

What happened instead was that both private citizens and corporations were ruined financially, several industries required governmental bailouts, and a number of major banks and financial institutions ceased to exist. Many Americans lost their life savings that had been invested in 401k plans or Individual Retirement Accounts (IRAs), and unlike the dotcom bubble, the financial crisis of 2008 impacted all areas and levels of society. "Prior to the repeal of Glass-Steagall in 1998, the market had had regular crashes that did not spill over into the real economy" (Ritholtz, 2009, p. xxvi), but the 2008 crisis did exactly that. In many cases, the individuals affected did not even know that their money had been invested in the stock market. Companies lost entire pension accounts, leaving retired employees with no funds. Governments of many small towns and communities, long known for the eagerness to invest in the stock market, were also greatly impacted. Town budgets suddenly were depleted of funds for infrastructure improvements, payments for adequate law enforcement, and money for schools and other institutions. Even the family of the author of this thesis was affected by the crisis. Essentially, "those who had put their faith in the free market, lifelong savings were erased in one fell swoop" (Chossudovsky and Marshall, 2010, p. 8).

We look back at the financial crisis of 2008 with determination never to let such a disaster happen again. Despite this, no special precautions have been put in place to prevent another financial crisis like the one in 2008. While the calls to re-enact Glass-Steagall grow louder and stronger, banks and other financial institutions continue to engage in questionable investment practices. Without the Glass-Steagall Act, many do so completely without constraints. "The repeal of Glass-Steagall could very well end up being the single most costly legislative repeal in the nation's history" (Ritholtz, 2009, p. 137). Even today, some in the financial sector argue that "the principles and the methods by which Glass-Steagall worked in the past… will work now to open this possibility of investment in economic recovery, to clean away the trash, of many, many trillions of dollars of unpayable debt" (Ogden, 2015, p. 22).

3. A FULL-BLOWN CRISIS

By 2008, globalization was in full swing, banks and other financial institutions basically had for years had the freedom to invest assets as they desired, and the overall feeling had been that of an economic upswing. Mortgages were very easy to obtain, property was considered to be an attractive investment, and banks and other financial institutions flourished, especially the larger ones. However, it is important to keep in mind that there were many negative events happening simultaneously. The U.S. War with Iraq had been raging for six years with no end in sight, U.S. troops had been deployed in Afghanistan since the Word Trade Center and Pentagon attacks of 2001, the price of crude oil had skyrocketed to nearly $160 per barrel, and the U.S was facing increased competition from China and the European Union in both trade and international influence. Many financial experts might even argue that the situation was ripe for a major event such as the Great Recession, and more and more people could see that "the potential for financial Armageddon was unconsciously enormous" (Ritholtz, 2009, p. 141).

Recessions are very difficult to define and it is not always clear when a nation is going through one. Economists often struggle to differentiate between an economic slowdown and an actual recession. Financial experts are very reluctant to use the 'R-word', instead arguing that a recession is simply a financial market correcting itself. In any case, the end result is usually that the economy significantly worsens, job hunting becomes more difficult and complex, profits decline, wages stagnate, and there are more bankruptcies. Recessions, though not as severe as depressions, can inflict a great deal of damage on a country's citizens and more importantly lead to a decline or even lack of confidence in a country's markets. This is exactly what transpired in 2008, the year it all came to a sudden halt, even though the run-up to the crisis was actually much longer than that, beginning almost ten years earlier and having many contributing factors. Experts "thought [they] knew enough to keep that from happening again" (Krugman, 2009, p. 4), and they "already had models that told [them] the crisis was coming" (Mirowski, 2014, p. 270). However, only fools fail to see the obvious. In hindsight, "economists mostly failed to predict the worst economic crisis since the 1930s" (*ibid.*, p. 246).

That housing and property prices usually go up in value is a well-known fact. Historically, investing in real estate has also been considered a prudent move. Property prices have soared over the past century in nearly every country on earth, in step with the ever-increasing global population, soon to reach eight billion. Land is subject to the laws of supply and demand: the more people needing property and housing, the greater demand, and therefore the higher the price. The first decade of the 21st century proved to be no exception to this rule.

The Great Recession began during this decade. The recession, arguably having started 2006 with the bursting of the U.S housing market bubble, would earn the rare distinction of being a truly global recession[9]. By 2006, real-estate prices had already gone through the roof and talk of a bubble was circulating. When the bubble did finally burst in 2006, the financial sector feigned surprise at first, in spite of all the red flags that had been visible for years.

Real estate bubbles had happened before in many countries and even in the U.S. However, nothing had prepared the U.S. for a bubble of this magnitude and scope. It was a home-grown crisis about to go global. In 2008, while real estate bubbles had not yet burst in other countries, the U.S. burst would signify the onset of a chain-reaction in global real estate markets. Country by country, bubbles burst, and the degree at which each country's economy was affected depended on a myriad of national and regional factors.

The U.S. housing bubble had its roots in a number of questionable practices. These practices include – but are certainly not limited to – banks offering subprime mortgages to individuals with questionable credit histories

---

[9] The crisis had fulfilled various criteria set out by the International Monetary Fund, primarily the per-capita decline in real world GDP.

(often with no down payment)[10], trading in mortgage-backed securities, risky loans, and greatly over-inflated asset prices. Basically, bank employees developed increasingly risky behavior that would eventually have an impact on the entire market. This risky behavior – leading to above-normal short-term returns – was not only strongly encouraged by the banks and financial institutions themselves, but was even heavily rewarded with promotions, huge bonuses, and recognition. Legal or not, this is precisely the risky behavior that was prohibited in the Glass-Steagall Act of 1933. It states that:

> no member bank shall act as the medium or agent of any non-banking corporation, partnership, association, business trust, or individual in making loans on the security of stocks, bonds, and other investment securities to brokers or dealers in stocks, bonds, and other investment securities (Carpenter et al., online, accessed 2017-01-06).

Despite being prohibited by Glass-Steagall and illegal up to that point, this activity now became common, spreading like a virus, attacking most financial institutions, whether they be banks, S&Ls, or simple investors.

It should be noted that during the years leading up to the Great Recession, more people became homeowners than at any other time in recorded history. In a perfect

---

[10] The Federal Reserve lowered interest rates during the recession of 1991-92 and again in 2001-02. These actions were designed to encourage banks to lend more money, especially in the form of subprime and adjustable-rate mortgages. These mortgages were designed to help people with little money and few assets acquire property.

world, this would have been considered a positive development. Prices for every type of real estate had begun to rise steadily and were valued at never before seen prices, leading many to believe that the purchasing of the real estate was an exceptional investment with very few risks[11]. Moreover, from 2000 to 2006, the total estimated values of property rose from $21 trillion to $30.5 trillion. Everyone wanted in on the game. Mortgages were never easier to obtain, and for many people it seemed that banks were literally giving them away. Even "second mortgages became commonplace, and home equity loans were used to pay credit card bills" (Chossudovsky and Marshall, 2010, p. 64). People were encouraged to buy now, pay later, and a never-ending credit circle was created: Invest in real-estate, watch the value of the home increase and equity grow, refinance, then use the money to buy whatever. What could possibly go wrong?

For the vast majority of Americans, the ownership of a home is considered the be the biggest investment that is ever made, and for most "Americans, their home is their largest asset" (Ritholtz, 2009, p. 98).

In the not so distant past, one had to qualify for a mortgage, and the mortgage was not always easy to obtain, as

> the basis for making a mortgage loan to a potential home buyer has relied on several simple factors: Banks looked at the home buyer's employment

---

[11] This wave of speculation drove real estate prices higher, which in turn attracted more speculation. This raised prices and created a bubble.

> history and income, the size of the down payment, and the person's credit rating to determine the borrower's ability to service the debt (Ritholtz, 2009, p. 102).

By 2006 this had changed. During the real-estate boom of the early 2000s, "the basis for mortgage lending was no longer the borrower's ability to pay – it was the lender's ability to securitize and repackage a mortgage" (Ritholtz, 2009, p. 102). In other words, the qualifications that had been put in place and helped for many years were no longer required to obtain a mortgage. Down payments, once an important mortgage requirement, in many cases disappeared and mortgages were granted without a personal investment. In fact, "forty-three percent of first-time home buyers in 2005 put no money down" (Ritholtz, 2009, p. 129). Add to this the unfortunate phenomenon of granting mortgages at subprime rates, and what appears is a recipe for total disaster. "Some [independent mortgage brokers] developed an expertise in home buyers who did not quite meet the high standards of the major banks. Borrowers with lesser bona fides were considered subprime" (*ibid.*, p. 120). These mortgages, based on their risky nature, were sold at higher interest rates, for a higher premium, and to a great extent to minorities that had been previously ineligible for such credit. "Given the inability of subprime borrowers to get a prime loan, along with the increased risk of default due to the weaker ratios, these lenders were able to charge a premium for their services" (*ibid.*, p. 120). Moreover, "there was a reason why some people in the past had been denied credit: They could not afford the homes they tried to purchase" (*ibid.*, p. 146). This was no longer the case in the United States. Mortgages had never been easier to get in the entire history of the nation.

Graph 5: U.S. Subprime Lending Expanded Significantly 2004-2006

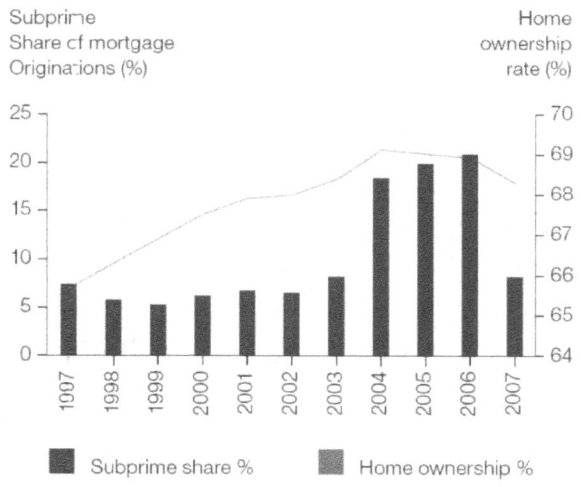

Source: Treasury Today, online, accessed 2017-11-06.

Banks saw an easy opportunity and immediately jumped on it. By granting mortgages to unqualified applicants, they could essentially increase their profits. It cost the subprime borrower much more to borrow the same amount of money than others at the prime rate, and they would subsequently end up paying extra to receive that mortgage. Banks were literally standing in line for the chance to make more such deals. By doing so, "they lent to unqualified borrowers, fed the derivatives market, and ultimately helped bring about a disaster – in housing, in subprime mortgages, and in mortgage-backed securities. This was the epicenter of the credit crisis" (Ritholtz, 2009, p. 128).

Refinancing also became more popular than ever. In the U.S., it had not been uncommon for a homeowner to have a second or third mortgage, and because housing prices had increased steadily for what had seemed like forever, home owners could trade some or all of their equity from the additional mortgage to buy additional things such as an automobile or home furnishings. By 2006, "second mortgages [had] became commonplace, and home equity loans were [even] used to pay credit card bills" (Chossudovsky and Marshall, 2010, p. 64). "The more Americans bought, the more they fell into debt. But as long as they had a house their false sense of security remained; their home was their equity, it would always go up in value, and they could always remortgage at lower rates if needed" (*ibid.*, p. 64).

However, with the disappearance of the down payment, there was less equity to be used. and when the real estate bubble finally burst, what little equity there had been had all but vanished. Considering then that "the typical family has a rather small percentage of their net worth in equities" (Ritholtz, 2009, p. 98), families became strapped for cash as their personal debt soared to unforeseen heights. Spending was not curtailed, and soon, "homeowners, long maxed out on their credit, were now beginning to default on their mortgages" (Chossudovsky and Marshall, 2010, p. 66). Individuals found themselves unable to pay these mortgages, and foreclosures became the norm. This situation applied especially to adjustable rate mortgages (ARMs), as "subprime adjustable-rate mortgages have had the highest foreclosure rates of all mortgages" (Ritholtz, 2009, p. 129). Additionally, "subprime mortgage-backed securities were the culmination of the growing usurpation by private American banks of power – not merely over the economy of the United States, but over the economy of the entire world" (Engdahl, 2010, p. 8).

To make matters worse, "in 2008, housing prices began to slide precipitously downwards and mortgages were suddenly losing value" (Chossudovsky and Marshall, 2010, p. 66). Equity disappeared, and home actually declined significantly in value. "The U.S. housing market went into a sharp downturn, and rates on Adjustable Rate Mortgages (ARMs) started moving sharply higher across the country" (Engdahl, 2010, p. 332).

Graph 6: Subprime Losses

Subprime losses — The 15 largest subprime serving companies in 2008:

Rank	Servicer (parent)	2Q 2008 servicing volume, in billions	Percent Change from 2Q 2007
1	Countrywide Financial (Bank of America)	$98.86	-21.4
2	HSBC Finance (HSBC)	80.48	-9.0
3	Chase Home Finance (JPMorgan Chase)	67.20	-17.7
4	Wells Fargo Home Mortgage (Wells Fargo)	49.35	-5.4
5	American Home Mortgage (WL Ross & Co.)	49.00	-24.9
6	Ocwen Financial Corp.	44.83	-15.6
7	Litton (Goldman Sachs)	44.10	-5.0
8	Home Loan Services (Bank of America)	44.00	-19.1
9	HomEq Mortgage Servicing (Barclays)	39.63	-21.0
10	Washington Mutual (JPMorgan Chase)	38.03	-30.7
11	Residential Capital LLC (GMAC)	31.13	-35.2
12	Saxon Mortgage (Morgan Staney)	30.00	-21.3
13	Citi (Citigroup)	22.94	-46.8
14	American General Finance (AIG)	19.45	5.3
15	EMC Mortgage (Bear Stearns/JPMorgan Chase)	19.43	-20.5

Source: The Big Picture, online, accessed 2017-11-06.

Some borrowers, upon applying for a second or third mortgage, were aghast to find that there was no equity to borrow against. Homeowners suddenly found themselves paying off mortgages that were valued much higher than the home itself. "As home prices declined, borrowers with adjustable-rate mortgages could not refinance to avoid the higher payments associated with rising interest rates. They began to default" (*ibid.*, p. 374), and "by September 2009, the number of home mortgages either in foreclosure process or one payment behind had risen to 14.4%, an historical record not seen since the statistics were begun in 1972" (*ibid.*, p. 374). Millions of American citizens soon discovered that "their financial lives were destroyed" (Warren, 2017, p. 36). Homeowners defaulted; banks foreclosed. "Home values were in free fall. Banks started auctioning off the homes to investors, who in turn rented them out to anyone who would have them" (Semuels,

2015, online, accessed 11-09-2017). Those who could afford housing elsewhere moved; others with nowhere to go became homeless.

In the case of foreclosures, once the homeowner had defaulted on mortgage payments, banks regained ownership of the afflicted properties. Whole neighborhoods emptied out, leaving behind shells of residences with plummeting values. "There are hundreds of stories of failed subdivisions left empty by the housing bust, where homeowners are stuck staring into vacant lots of PVC pipes and weeds" (Semuels, 2015, online, accessed 11-09-2017). Entire housing developments were left half-finished and unoccupied; in some cases, incomplete developments were even repurposed as farmland or grazing land for livestock. Some houses and properties could not even be given away. Real estate offices laid off employees or simply went out of business. "Millions of high-paid construction and white-collar real estate-related jobs vanished overnight" (Engdahl, 2010, p. 375). Experts still argue whether the Glass-Steagall Act could have prevented the 2008 housing crisis. However, when one considers that "the vast majority of subprime mortgage loans were made not by depository banks, but by unregulated nonbank lenders" (Ritholtz, 2009, p. xxvii), and it was "indiscriminate lending by mortgage originators [that] helped inflate the housing boom" (*ibid.*, p. 128),

Graph 7: Mortgage Delinquencies by Loan Type

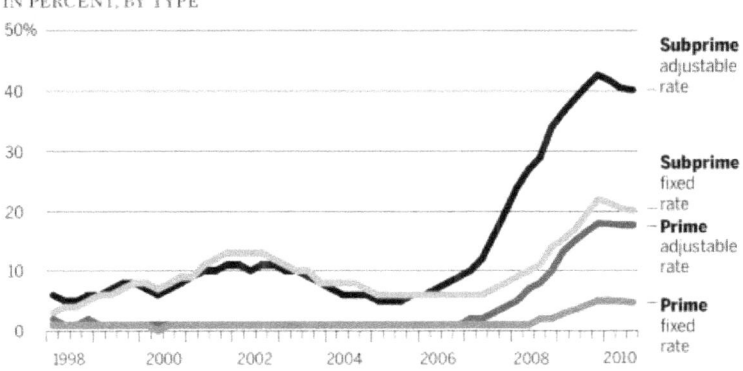

Source: Zero Hedge, online, accessed 2017-11-10.

one can only imagine what would have happened had the Glass-Steagall Act still been in place.

In any case, the offering of mortgages might have been permitted by Glass-Steagall, but the mortgages used as an investment tool would not have been allowed. "The combination of ultralow rates, new types of exotic mortgages, changes in lending standards, and massive securitization created the perfect storm for a housing boom" (*ibid.*, p. 90). This was fully taken advantage of by bankers with questionable behavior. This questionable behavior subsequently led to the investment in credit default swaps that would dominate the 2008 banking crisis, leading to bailouts unimagined by economists at the time.

Banks were getting rich at the expense of their customers, and

> from the crash onward, it was bad enough to endure house prices sinking under water, dangling defaults and foreclosures, the collapse of what remained of manufacturing employment, the reduction of whole neighborhoods to bombed-out shells, the evaporation of pensions and savings accounts, the dismay of witnessing the hope of a better life for our children shrivel up, neighbors stocking up on firearms and people confusing bankruptcy with the Rapture (Mirowski, 2014, p. 1).

4. THE TOOLS OF A CRISIS

From the point of view of the banks and lending institutions, foreclosures were exceptionally good business. Essentially, "Bankruptcies and foreclosures constitute a money-spinning operation for the financial giants" (Chossudovsky and Marshall, 2010, p. 10). Offering subprime mortgages to those who would struggle to repay them also constituted abuse. "There are numerous examples of lenders deceptively convincing borrowers to agree to loan terms that are abusive" (Ritholtz, 2009, p. 123). Mortgage lenders knew that the likelihood of repayment of the subprime mortgages that they had pushed on applicants was very low. Only the borrowers themselves were unaware of this, as "they were lying to themselves as they financially engineered their way into homes they couldn't afford" (*ibid.*, p. 129).

4.1 Subprime Mortgages

Subprime mortgages soon became a very popular business model, and "the formula was [incredibly] simple: first, make a fortune by tricking families into signing on to really lousy mortgages; next, make another fortune by bundling those mortgages together and selling them to unsuspecting pension funds and municipalities; and finally, when it all blows up, go to the government for a gigantic handout" (Warren, 2017, p. 38). All along, mortgage lenders were planning to land on their two feet; it was the borrower that would suffer the dire consequences. Many had lost their jobs, were already deep in debt, and "a lousy mortgage made a bad situation worse" (*ibid.*, p. 34). Foreclosures, in some cases, were even welcomed by the borrower, offering some financial relief. However, sometimes even a foreclosure did not offer the expected debt relief because

> with mortgage defaults, banks seize and resell the home. But if a degree can't be sold, that doesn't deter the banks. They essentially wrote the student loan law in which the fine-print says they aren't 'dischargeable.' So even if you file for bankruptcy, the payments continue due (Mirowski, 2014, p. 138).

This meant that a borrower was on the hook for the mortgage even long after losing the house on which the mortgage in question was based. "Mortgage firms set about to ignore long-standing legal restrictions on conveyance and foreclosure" (Mirowski, 2014, p. 85). Never before had the residential landscape of the United States been so altered and the American dream of owning a house so shattered.

4.2 Credit Default Swaps

By 2008, the derivatives known as credit default swaps[12] had become the one of the most popular investment tools among banks. They had already been popular since October 2004, after "the Securities and Exchange Commission agreed to waive regulations on five of the biggest [banks]… allowing them to invest more in these risky mortgage-backed securities" Sass, Pearson, and Hattikudur, 2011, chapter 10, paragraph 40). A questionable practice indeed, they were actually "challenged as being illegal in the 1990s, [and] Greenspan legalized the derivatives practice" (Chossudovsky and Marshall, 2010, p. 65). Credit default swaps were essentially bets, and "these bets had absolutely no value whatsoever and were not investments. They were just financial instruments called derivatives – high stakes gambling" (*ibid.*, p. 65). They could include as assets any loan amount (in some cases blocks of hundreds, even thousands of loans) owed to them. To fool the ratings agencies, banks "deliberately mixed bad loans with good loans in securities, making the risks appear less risky than they actually were" (Sass, Pearson, and Hattikudur, 2011, chapter 10, paragraph 52). A few isolated cases would not

[12] A credit default swap is a financial phenomenon in which the seller of the swap owes compensation to the buyer should the mortgage or other loan end in default.

have made much of a difference, but the banks and other institutions simply saw this as a new and very lucrative form of investment. "The volume of risky mortgage-backed securities issued annually rose from $87 billion in 2001 to $450 billion in 2006" (*ibid.*, chapter 10, paragraph 42). Anyone could see that "banks had built an entire financial universe on the unworthy foundations of subprime mortgages" (*ibid,* chapter 10, paragraph 36.).

Credit default swaps were certainly not illegal, but before the crisis, they were not as common as one might believe. As a matter of fact, it was assumed that "banks use the CDS market largely to hedge their credit exposure" (Minton, Stulz, and Williamson, 2009, online, accessed 2017-09-05). The problem with credit default swaps was that they became popular very fast. And nearly no one expected the activity in question to reach the point where it impacted the economy in the way it did. Derivatives created a lot of problems before and during the Great Recession. Add to this already complicated situation the fact that

> the largest banks became entirely interconnected with one another, particularly through making derivative bets, and therefore having the same derivatives exposures; while their leverage ratios – their assets to capital – was allowed to rise from 16:1 as a typical ratio to 30:35. And their loans fell to about half of their total assets; they stopped lending to the businesses and households while they got so much rapidly larger (Ogden, 2015, p. 15-16).

Uncoupling the derivatives from the banks in question would be no easy task.

While life for most Americans had been turned upside down, mortgage lenders were simply ecstatic by the developments. "To guarantee, therefore, these high-risk mortgages, the same financial houses that sold them then created 'insurance policies' against the sub-prime investments they were selling, marketed as Credit Default Swaps (CDS)" (Chossudovsky and Marshall, 2010, p. 65).

These credit default swaps were then bundled together and sold as a package to others as an investment tool. Thus, mortgage lenders were getting paid for issuing the mortgage and by the insurance company if and when the mortgage failed. Essentially, they were hedging their bets and were paid regardless of whether there had actually been a foreclosure on the home or property.

4.3 Faulty Ratings

What surprised nearly all Americans was that the ratings agencies played along with the whole deal. "Not only did the initial ratings prove to be too generous, but the agencies were much too slow in downgrading housing-related bonds when mortgage defaults and foreclosures started to rise" (Ritholtz, 2009, p. 112). These ratings agencies had been long respected as "most fixed-income products come with a grade from one of three major rating agencies" (*ibid.*, p. 111), Moody's, Fitch, or Standard and Poor's. These "three rating agencies dominated the global business of credit ratings, the largest in the world being Moody's Investor Service." (Engdahl, 2010, p. 324). Not only did the ratings agencies completely ignore some of the questionable behavior demonstrated by banks, by not acting they essentially condoned the behavior, and "turned a blind eye to the inherent risk of the products" (Engdahl, 2010, p. 348). In many cases, they even rewarded the questionable investment activities with the highest possible rating: Triple-A. Normally, "triple-A is the most creditworthy rating; this grade is only given (in theory) to the highest-quality borrowers, such as the U.S. government and top companies" (Ritholtz, 2009, p. 111). The institutions investing in the derivatives in question were neither high-quality nor U.S. government. They were simply paid to rate them so highly. Ratings agencies "slapped their highest ratings on paper that was actually junk. They did so because investment banks paid them to" (*ibid.*, p. xxv). On paper, the derivatives looked like a sure bet, when in reality they were worth very little. This gross malpractice by the three ratings agencies "was a fatal abuse of their unique regulatory role" (*ibid.*, p. xxv), and contributed greatly to the overall financial crisis.

When it comes to the Great Recession of 2008, there is enough blame to go around: "The mortgage broker who fudges the load application, the bank that looks the other way to process it, and the fund manager that ultimately buys this crappy paper are all focused not on sustainable, long-term returns, but on the quick buck" (*ibid.*, p. 5). Basically, it all comes down to how to make as much profit in the short-term and completely disregard the long-term.
"The skewed compensation scheme at banks and investment houses paid senior employees huge bonuses for short-term profits despite longer-term liabilities" (Ritholtz, 2009, p. xxvii). Risks were completely and utterly ignored: "The ordinary liability and risk that is supposed to go with investing and business ventures seems to have disappeared" (*ibid.*, p. 4). Banking ethics hit an all-time low.

An interesting angle is that the banks in question must have known that something was terribly awry. Even a

normal citizen not involved in any way in the financial sector knows that high risk usually brings high returns. At the other end of the spectrum are the lower risk investments that bring nowhere near the same returns as the default credit swaps did. The signs were always clearly there, and plain to see, yet so many *chose* not to see them. Not only did the banks and other financial institutions know about the high default risk of credit default swaps,
they simply ignored the obvious risk, even paying out huge bonuses to those individuals who were most active in the credit default swap scheme. This is the case even despite the fact that by September 2008, more than 9 percent of all mortgages in the U.S. were in a default status.

5. THE FAILURE OF GIANTS

So, "how did the United States of America get into such a predicament whereby in one year, 2008, the financial system nearly vaporized, the stock market crashed, real estate tanked, and major corporations were being bailed out (or begging to be) on a regular basis" (Ritholtz, 2009, p. viii)? Very few people saw it coming, and when it all came crashing down, a few of the players – big banks that should have seen the red flags – came down with it. Bear-Stearns was one of the first to go, and "when [it] fell apart, few suspected a cascading collapse across the entire financial firmament. Yet that is precisely what occurred" (*ibid.*, p. 185). Financial experts were left scratching their heads while the end of Bear-Stearns "set the stage for the worst financial crisis since the Great Depression" (*ibid.*, p. xxi). The first giant had fallen, stumbling to his knees. How many more would follow?

Next in line was Lehman Brothers. Lehman Brothers Holdings had been a fixture in the American financial sector since the year 1850, and with more than 20,000 employees, it was one of the largest employers in the sector. However, on "Friday, September 12, 2008, Lehman Brothers faced collapse in weekend negotiations behind closed doors on Wall Street... filing for Chapter 11 bankruptcy by Lehman on Monday morning"

(Chossudovsky and Marshall, 2010, p. 4). A company that had lasted more than 150 years was gone in a matter of days. "Equity markets were in free fall" (Ritholtz, 2009 p. xxi), and no one knew where it would end. Soon another large institution disappeared: "Wachovia Bank was taken over by Wells Fargo, overriding a competing bid from Citigroup" (Chossudovsky and Marshall, 2010, p. 6). To some people it appeared that a few big fish were drowning while other big fish were devouring the little fish in a battle for survival of the fittest.

Sure enough, "the following day, it was the turn of AIG, the insurance conglomerate" (Chossudovsky and Marshall, 2010, p. 4), to fail. The world's largest insurance company would suffer the same fate as Bear-Stearns and Lehman Brothers. However, AIG handled the crisis differently: While it was going down, it continued to pay out bonuses to upper management and even refused to cancel team-building trips that had been scheduled for employees. These trips involved lavish hotels and other facilities with high-end entertainment costing millions of dollars. American taxpayers, still reeling from the collapse of the other big banks, did not take kindly to these events, and some members of congress accused AIG executives of trying to spend as much as they could, before being bailed out by the government. They were correct.

Then, another big bank failed. Merrill Lynch would follow in AIG's footsteps, paying out huge bonuses while the corporation was failing financially. However, things happened differently: "As events unfolded, Merrill Lynch was bought and Lehman Brothers was pushed into bankruptcy" (Chossudovsky and Marshall, 2010, p. 9).

Others would not be not so lucky. Washington Mutual was gobbled up by JPMorgan Chase, after being seized by the Office of Thrift Supervision. Mortgage Fannie Mae[13], a mortgage securities company founded during the Great Depression and its brother organization, Freddie Mac[14], soon went belly-up. The U.S. government felt that these two corporations deserved special consideration, but despite receiving assistance from the government, the two organizations slipped further into financial trouble, leading to their stock being delisted from the New York Stock Exchange in 2010. "Wachovia Bank was taken over by Wells Fargo, overriding a competing bid from Citigroup" (Chossudovsky and Marshall, 2010, p. 6).

Americans were "shocked by the total collapse of so many major financial firms, such as BearStearns, Countrywide Financial, Fannie Mae, and Freddy Mac in such a short amount of time" (Ritholtz, 2009, p. xiv).

Very few citizens remained untouched; it seemed that every person had a family member, friend, or acquaintance that was a customer of one of these financial institutions. People were losing faith in the

---

[13] Fannie Mae is an accepted abbreviation for the Federal National Mortgage Association.

[14] Freddie Mac is an accepted abbreviation for the Federal Home Loan Mortgage Corporation

system, and worse: they were losing trust. "Banks are wonderful things, when they work. And they usually do. But when they don't, all hell can break loose" (Krugman, 2009, p. 153). All hell had broken loose, and the U.S. government would soon be required to restore order to a system that had run rampant for more than a few years. The real question would be the cost of restoring the trust of American taxpayers in the financial sector, trust that been so blatantly abused. How much more could the American public take? How many other sectors of the economy would be affected by the banking and real-estate crises? It turns out that the manufacturing sector would be the next target.

Graph 8: Stockmarket Losses During Selected Financial Crises

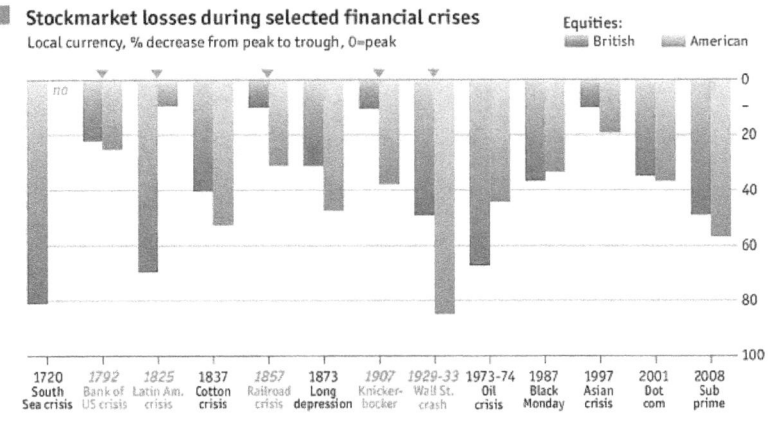

Source: *The Telegraph, online, accessed 2017-11-06.*

An old English adage tell us that hindsight is 20/20. Ever since the crisis, "from the failure of Bear Stearns [going] forward, journalists scrambled to understand how it could be that problems in one sector would ramify and amplify into other sectors, such that the entire financial system seemed poised on the brink of utter failure" (Mirowski, 2014, p. 168). Panic was everywhere. It was very clear that "this crisis is far more serious than the Great Depression. All major sectors of the global economy are affected" (*ibid.*, p. 4). With the stock market losing value, "the snowballing instability then becomes cumulative, leading to an overall slide of market values" (*ibid.*, p. 8). Over the course of the crisis, "the Dow Jones crashed more than 7,600 points to about 6,500 by the time it bottomed in March 2009" (Ritholtz, 2009, p. xxi).

Manufacturing was also hit hard. Many companies had to lay off employees to stop the losses. Millions now found themselves jobless, with little prospect of finding new employment. "The economic recession [was] deep-seated, resulting in mass unemployment, the collapse of state social programs and the impoverishment of millions of people" (Chossudovsky and Marshall, 2010, p. xv). Soon it became obvious to all that the crisis at hand was in fact "the most dramatic catastrophic global economic collapse after the Great Depression of the 1930s" (Mirowski, 2014, p. 2). Moreover, it hadn't even begun to taper off. There was much more to come.

5.1 The Auto Industry Crisis

Virtually no part of the U.S. economy remained unaffected by the Great Recession. The financial crisis of 2008 affected many industries, including the U.S. automobile industry. General Motors and other auto manufactures soon found themselves in very dire financial situations indeed. Moreover, the crisis cost the U.S. $648 billion due to slower economic growth, $3.4 trillion in real estate wealth, $7.4 trillion in stock wealth, and 5.5 million jobs (Swagel, 2010, online, accessed 2017-01-06). Additionally, there was "a dearth of buyers either holding tight to their cash as a hedge against possible job loss or unable to obtain loans from banks fearful of collapse" (Binder, 2009, online, accessed 2017-09-20), and this affected the number of new cars sold. "Add a third year of skyrocketing summer fuel prices, and the resulting sales decline leads a number of the world's top auto makers to seek government assistance, with at least two fighting for their corporate lives by year's end" (Binder, 2009, online, accessed 2017-09-20). The population of the U.S. was already in very bad shape; the automakers were in worse condition. To put things into the proper perspective, "U.S. households lost on average nearly $5,800 in income due to reduced economic growth during the acute stage of the financial crisis from September 2008 through the end of

2009" (Swagel, 2010, online, accessed 2017-01-06). This essentially meant less money to buy fewer cars.

By late 2008, the U.S. government had been taking notice of the growing crisis in the automobile manufacturing sector. Already, "world vehicle production in 2008 totaled 69,399,929 units, down 4.1% from the record 72,318,416 built the previous year. Although still the industry's second-best performance in history, it is one that auto makers will be hard pressed to repeat in 2009, with significant sales declines forecast for major markets" (Binder, 2009, online, accessed 2017-09-20). The stock market was hit by decreasing automobile sales. "Ford's shares dived by 8% while GM's stock slumped by 6.7%. The slump in motoring stocks, together with fresh fears of losses at leading banks, contributed to a gloomy mood on Wall Street as the Dow Jones Industrial Average dropped 220 points to 11,842" (Clark, 2008, online, accessed 2017-09-20). In the eyes of many, the only way in which the U.S. would be able to recover was to bail out most of those corporations that were affected. A major bailout, specific to the automobile industry was suggested, as it is a major driver of the U.S. economy and the failure of any of the three largest automobile manufacturers would have a significant impact on the overall health of the U.S. "Solving the auto industry problems is an opportunity to begin to shape a more effective new economy that changes the relationship between corporations and government as well as shares the wealth more equitably" (Zeese, 2008, online, accessed 2017-09-20).

The reasons the automobile crises began are various. There were in fact many factors, but most agree that the major factors were employee benefits (including health care), inability for potential car buyers to get credit due to the problems in the credit market, and finally, the lagging of U.S.-made automobile behind their Asian and European competitors in both quality and efficiency. In other words, Americans didn't want the cars Detroit had made, the cars were difficult to obtain due to credit issues, and the automaker employers could not deliver the basic benefits package that had been promised to their employees.

Very few industries had reached the level of economic importance as the automotive industry. Ever since the automobile became the primary mode of transportation in the United States the automobile industry has been a major player in the country's economy. A major employer, employing more than eight million Americans, the automobile industry also represented 2.2 percent of the total GDP. Yet, while cries of "no bailout" could be heard from both sides of the political aisle and by many citizens, under no circumstances was the government willing to let the auto industry (as well as any other important industry) fail. Despite this, financial bailouts were very tricky business indeed. "The implications of this are significant. The current bout of bailouts – the banks and brokers, airlines and automakers, lenders and borrowers in the housing industry – will have long-lasting repercussions"

(Ritholtz, 2009, p. 6).

In 2008, the real question was how to go about rescuing the big three. It was obvious that the big three, General Motors, Ford, and Chrysler, would have to be bailed out at taxpayers' expense, but what guarantees did the American public have that the money would be repaid? The first step was to determine just how much would actually be needed to bail the manufacturers out. This number was certainly not easy to identify, as "there was evidence that the November 2008 plunge of the U.S. automobile industry was in part the result of financial manipulation" (Chossudovsky and Marshall, 2010, p. 10), so some numbers were not to be trusted. The government then "followed by deciding which auto firms and insurance companies would live or die" (Mirowski, 2014, p. 85). The automotive industry ultimately found itself in the hands of the U.S. government.

In exchange for financial assistance, a nicer term for a bailout, the auto makers would be required to submit to financial management by the U.S. government. The government saw this as "an opportunity to begin to re-make the relationship between corporations and government" (Zeese, 2008, online, accessed 2017-09-17). The Ford Motor Company almost immediately rejected the terms of the bailout and subsequently decided that they would not receive any government funds. The other two, General Motors and Chrysler, reluctantly accepted the bailout. Something would have to be done by the government to ensure that the automobile industry would be able to compete after the reins of control were handed back to their CEOs. This included dropping the traditional gas-guzzling American cars and start building smaller, sleeker models based on those Japan and Europe, that the "EPA estimates to get over 30 miles per gallon" (*ibid.*). The automobile industry was not at all happy with the new requirement, and "did not want to be told to build more efficient cars" (*ibid.*). However, they did start to build them, and the industry was turned around, seeing profits once again.

The Ford Motor Company decided to go it alone, declining participation in the bailout. This decision was made not because the company deemed itself strong enough to weather the financial crisis alone, but rather because management was not comfortable giving control over the company to the U.S. government. In the eyes of business leaders, government involvement meant more regulations. Ford was convinced that the suggested regulation would further impact the company's chance for survival. Ford's move also displayed more loyalty toward its shareholders than concern over the state of the nation's economy. Everyone knew that Ford was already betting on sales after the crisis. They hoped that American taxpayers would remember that Ford had not accepted bailout money, and that this would translate into sales of new automobiles. In hindsight, they were only partially correct.

5.2 Failure of the Fed

The Glass-Steagall Act could have prevented much of what happened before the Great Recession. The Fed could have also played a much bigger role in how the crisis played out, softening its impact. Furthermore, had the Gramm-Leach-Bliley Act not repealed Glass-Steagall, credit default swaps would have been prohibited, subprime mortgages would have been severely regulated, and banks would have not become the huge entities that they are today. Had all of these been addressed by an act still in place, the automotive industry would not have had to undergo the loss of sales based on inability of consumers to obtain credit for the purchasing of new cars.

The Fed was designed to help prevent crises of this magnitude. It had already known that something was awry. Actions that sparked the 2008 financial crisis were not limited to the United States, but were commonplace around the globe, and
> based on data for roughly 1,000 bank and nonbank financial institutions – including insurance companies, investment banks and asset managers – in 22 countries over the past 15 years, [we found] significant evidence of increased risk-taking behavior. Domestic banks and nonbanks alike increase their leverage ratios in response to

> persistent monetary policy accommodation at home. In addition, prolonged Federal Reserve policy easing leads banks and nonbanks outside the U.S. to take on more risks, with an effect similar to equivalent domestic monetary policies (Cecchetti et al., 2017, p. 19).

The Fed did not only fail to prevent, but its actions of easing its monetary policies further worsened the crisis, the opposite of what its purpose is. Other entities abroad were also forced to scramble, picking up whatever pieces they could.

The 2008 financial crisis is one example of how many events in one country can have a global impact. Going forward, this domino effect must be considered when high-risk actions are taken by any individual or institution, regardless of economic sector.

6. THE BAILOUTS

In 2008, when outgoing President George W. Bush announced his plans to bailout some of the larger banks, critics everywhere were outraged. This is precisely when the phrase "too big to fail"[15] was born. Initially, the bailout consisted of the "$700 billion that the treasury department used to save the banks during the financial crash in September of 2008" (Collins, 2015, online, accessed 2017-01-06), and was intended to buy back mortgage-backed securities from the bank. However, this was only the beginning. The bailout soon became known as TARP (Troubled Assets Recovery Program), and the term was used so often that it soon became commonplace. TARP was huge, and "the Special Inspector General for TARP summary of the bailout says that the total commitment of government is $16.8 trillion dollars with the $4.6 trillion already paid out" (Collins, 2015, online, accessed 2017-01-06).

"The groundwork for modern bailouts was laid in the early twentieth century, when in 1913, the Federal Reserve System was created" (Ritholtz, 2009, p. 10).

---

[15] 'Too big to fail' was a phrase used often during the bailouts of 2008 to refer to banks that were so important to a country's financial well-being that a bankruptcy or failure by these institutions would result in major implications for the country.

However, never before had the U.S. government done so much to help industries that had been negatively affected by the deeds of a few individuals and corporations. The only actions that even came close were responses to natural disasters. "The bailout measures under the Bush and Obama administrations have contributed to a further process of destabilization of the financial architecture" (Chossudovsky and Marshall, 2010, p. 24).

6.1 Saving the Banks

As already mentioned, two major financial institutions, Bear Stearns and Lehman Brothers had already failed, but other financial institutions soon took full advantage of the U.S. government's plan to bail them out of the financial crisis. This completely polarized the American people. "The United States has had several distinct bailout eras, and each has seen an incremental shift in the attitudes toward government rescues" (Ritholtz, 2009, p. 9). Many saw it as the only solution to the financial crisis and a perfectly good way to curb the disastrous consequences of the Great Recession, which at the time the event was already being called. Others saw it as a ridiculous reaction to a real problem, not unlike "pouring gasoline on a fire," and by no means a permanent solution to the problem. Moreover, "since the 1990s, bailouts have been embraced around the world as a near-normal responsibility of government to save the financial markets from themselves" (*ibid.*, p. 9). They complained that the U.S. government, by bailing out the major banks, was essentially

> committing American taxpayers to permanent, blind support of an ungovernable, unregulatable, hyper concentrated new financial system that exacerbates the greed and inequality that caused

the crash, and forces Wall Street banks like Goldman Sachs and Citigroup to increase risk rather than reduce it (Collins, 2015, online, accessed 2017-01-06).

They were also concerned that it would lead to banks taking even greater risks going forward. If banks knew that they would be protected against failure by the U.S. government, what was there to lose by practicing such risky behavior? This was unacceptable to some, and "many suggested to just let the markets run their course. That would have created a global depression, as businesses around the world shut down due to lack of credit. That would have caused large-scale unemployment and a downward economic spiral." (Amadeo, online, accessed 2017-01-06).

6.2 Rescuing the Automakers

The auto industry, which was greatly affected by the Great Recession, was also given a huge bailout by the U.S. government. Since the late 1940s, the U.S. government had considered the auto industry to be an economic driver, critical to the financial success of the nation. It could even be argued that his group has been given preferential treatment over the years, much to the dismay of other

Table 1: Bailout Figures for Major U.S. Automakers

Company	Sold For	Invested	Bailout Ended
GM	$39.7 bill.	$51 bill.	December 9, 2013
GMAC (Ally)	$19.6 bill.	$17 bill.	December 18, 2014
Chrysler	$11.2 bill.	$12.5 bill.	May 2011
TOTAL	$70.5 billion	$80.7 bill.	

Source: The Balance, online, accessed 2017-01-20.

industries that are just as important.

The so-call 'Big Three'[16] automakers met with congress in early 2009 to discuss the details of the bailout. While Ford declined the U.S. government's offer of a bailout, General Motors, GMAC, and Chrysler graciously accepted

---

[16] The "Big Three" refers to the largest automobile manufacturers in the United States: General Motors (GM), Ford Motor Company, and Chrysler.

the bailout and the conditions applicable to it. The bailout was structured as follows:

As can be seen in the above table, the total bailout of the U.S. automotive industry totaled $80.7 billion. One of the criteria of the bailout was for the automakers to cede management of their companies to the U.S. government, at least for a period of time. Although they were reluctant to give up control, the automobile manufacturers finally did agree to the conditions of the bailout. It is a good thing they did. Chrysler ended up merging with Italy's Fiat, which gave it new life, and "in June 2009, GM and Chrysler emerged from bankruptcy. The bailout helped them create 340,000 additional jobs" (Amadeo, online, accessed 2017-01-08), and they were suddenly able to produce more efficient cars, something the public had been requesting for years. One can only imagine what might have happened had the Big Three not agree to the government's demands.

Years after the bailouts, the Big Three are once again profitable, although there still remains the risk that it could all happen again. The automobile industry is still too reliant on credit and banks, as most Americans take out a loan to purchase a new car. Also, car dealers are once again offering cars with no down payment, which is exactly what the lenders of sub-prime mortgages were doing before the crisis began. Hopefully, different results will follow.

6.3 Glass-Steagall and Bailouts

"The Fed made loans... to financial institutions at negligible rates of interest, with no quid pro quo" (Mirowski, 2014, p. 185). While the Glass-Steagall Act, had it still been in place, would not have had any impact on the number of bailouts, the industries that received them, or the actual amount of money paid by the U.S. government, it would have prevented a lot of the activity that eventually led to bailouts. One of the major problems was that

> the largest banks became entirely interconnected with one another, particularly through making derivative bets, and therefore having the same derivatives exposures; while their leverage ratios – their assets to capital – was allowed to rise from 16:1 as a typical ratio to 30-35:1. And their loans fell to about half of their total assets; they stopped lending to the businesses and households while they got so much rapidly larger" (Ogden, 2015, p. 15-16).

In the end, when all was said and done, "the costs of the bailout package came to $3.25 trillion, triple the size of the original $700 billion rescue package" (Ritholtz, 2009, p. 222). This infuriated many in the nation. "The public was furious over the bailout and Congress was under a lot of public pressure to regulate [the banks]" (Warren, 2017, p. 170). Instead of learning the desired lesson taught by Glass-Steagall, "encouraging risk-taking to be separated from its consequences" (Ritholtz, 2009, p. 72), the only lesson that the bailed-out corporations "actually learned was that the Fed (and by extension, Uncle Sam) would be there to back them up when they ran into trouble" (*ibid.*, p. 72). In the end, it all came down to accountability. "[Moral hazard] arises when an individual or institution does not bear the full consequences of its actions, and therefore tends to act less carefully than they otherwise would, leaving a third party to bear the responsibility for the consequences of those actions" (Ritholtz, 2009, p. 161). The United States will be dealing with those consequences for years to come.

7. CONCLUSION

An old saying, in its best-known form, states that looking back provides the most accurate vision possible. This adage can certainly be applied to the repeal of the Glass-Steagall Act in 1999, the Great Recession, and the subsequent bailouts by the U.S. government. Would the Glass-Steagall Act have prevented the 2008 financial crisis? Many outspoken economists believe so. Even those who do not strongly believe in Glass-Steagall preventing the crisis agree that the act, had it been in place, would have at least softened the impact. If it had been in place, "Glass-Steagall would have at least provided what the first of its names portends: transparency" (Engdahl, 2010, p. 318). Economic experts agree that "lack of transparency was at the root of the crisis that had finally and inevitably erupted by mid-2007" (*ibid.*, p. 348).

While the 2008 financial crisis almost certainly would have occurred if Glass-Steagall had not been repealed, the Gramm-Leach-Bliley Act and other deregulation greatly aided the spread of the disaster throughout the financial system and the broader economy. Unfortunately, even today, there's been too little willingness by those on Wall Street and in Washington to admit this mistake (and others) or, more importantly, to allow the facts to guide our efforts to prevent another financial crash. (Kelleher,

online, accessed 2017-01-06) The sad fact is that
> the lessons of the crisis were so manifestly obvious: Banks could not be trusted to regulate themselves; corporate managements cheat all the time (at least when they think they can get away with it); accounting statements are near worthless to investor; regulatory capture was everywhere; and Wall Street manages to find ways around all but the clearest, most stringent, black-letter regulations" (Ritholtz, 2009, p. xxii).

Yet that is exactly what banks were and are now being asked to do: regulate themselves. "Historically, excessive greed, recklessness, and foolish speculations were punished by the market" (Ritholtz, 2009, p. 4). The 2008 financial crisis demonstrated that this was no longer true.

However, going forward, the banks will no longer have the trust of the American people, and this will limit their ability to commit investment fraud. Americans will remember what happened to their assets when banks were left to run freely. Banks simply did not do an adequate job of regulating themselves. They never have, and never will. Banks will have to find other ways to regain the trust of U.S. investors, otherwise the public will look elsewhere to invest its money. Moreover, banks must understand that
> actions have consequences. Denying reality, falsifying data, gaming the numbers, cooking the books, making believe inflation is more modest than it really is, or pretending toxic assets deserve the highest credit ratings all have real-world

consequences, intended and otherwise (Ritholtz, 2009, p. 159).

The U.S. government needs to demand accountability from the banks. "The reason to demand some accountability is to make sure it won't happen again" (Warren, 2017, p. 238). History has shown us that "when giant banks weren't held to some basic rules and accountability, people got ripped off, risk-taking exploded, and markets blew up" (*ibid.*, p. 149). A lack of accountability leads to acceptance of fraudulent and abusive actions without fear of consequences or retribution. Banks certainly understand retribution, as they are usually the first to resort to disciplinary measures, issuing fines immediately when an account is overdrawn, or when bank processes and procedures are not properly followed. "America is [already] the most indebted country on earth. The United States (federal government) gross public debt is currently in the order of fourteen trillion dollars" (Chossudovsky and Marshall 2009, p. 52). Banks should not be in a position to make the matter worse.

While many believe that the 2008 financial crisis changed the banking culture, "contrary to every expectation, nothing much has been changed by the crash" (Mirowski, 2014, p. 8).
Today, banks are still too big to fail, even bigger than ever, as "more than 65 percent of the depositary assets are held by a handful of huge banks – and they are still less than stable" (Ritholtz, 2009, p. xxvi). These financial

behemoths will "continue to threaten our economy. The biggest banks are [even] much larger than they were before the crisis... and they continue to engage in dangerous practices that could once again crash our economy" (Ogden, 2015, p. 14). "Banks became too big to be effectively managed" (Ritholtz, 2009, p. 135-136).

However, the practices and daily investment activities of bank employees face much more scrutiny than in the past, and rightly so. It remains to be seen whether this scrutiny is enough to prevent their financial transgressions. On an entertaining note, "editorial cartoonists and TV comedians tried to turn the whole thing into a joke, portraying how buffoon bankers bemoaned that the restive public just could not understand that they were the only ones who could clean up the godawful mess they had made" (Mirowski, 2014, p. 9). For most Americans, the Great Recession was no joke. They are still trying to pick of the pieces of their lives and move on. Some have never recovered.

"While the risk of total economic collapse seems to be receding, that's a long way from saying that the crisis is over" (Krugman, 2009, p. 195). Yet, since the crisis, real-estate prices have again stabilized, and some parts of the United States are seeing reinvestment in half-finished housing projects that had been abandoned. Even some existing projects, finished before the Great Recession, have been continued. Homes are once again finding owners, and while "in 2010, there were 19 million vacant homes in the

United States – enough to house the population of France at 3.4 people per home" (Sass, Pearson, and Hattikudur, 2011, chapter 10, paragraph 38), this number has sharply decreased since the then. Property values have fallen to the reasonable levels of the pre-crisis era (experts would call this a correction), and investors are returning to the real-estate market in droves. The fall in property values may have also negatively affected the desire to invest in credit default swaps, making them less popular than they were before the crisis. Banks are now taking a much closer look at the credit histories of all mortgage applicants. The automobile industry, fueled by new investment, is once again profitable, and is once again a target of investors. The Dow-Jones Index has rebounded and is moving toward another important milestone: 20,000 points. There is a sense of well-being across the U.S. People are slowly starting to rebuild their retirement funds and lives, both of which were decimated by the 2008 crisis. "We survived, but that last financial bomb was nearly fatal for our economy – and for tens of millions of American families. We can't afford another hit" (Warren, 2017 p. 94).

The U.S. congress has even tried on several occasions to introduce Glass-Steagall-like legislation but has yet to be successful in enacting any law that would provide similar provisions. "The revival of Glass-Steagall is the single most urgent priority facing America" (Ingraham, 2015, p. 7).

Time will tell if the government has learned anything

from the Great Recession, and if it has the courage to address the factors that led up to the crisis.

There are many people out there – both experts and lay people – who completely disagree that the Glass-Steagall Act had any impact whatsoever on the likelihood of the crisis. Some financial experts in both the U.S. and around the globe believe that "Glass-Steagall was irrelevant to the financial crisis since it would not have affected the investment banks and commercial lenders that were distressed in 2008" (Hartley, 2015, online, accessed 2017-09-17). To these individuals, maintaining the *status quo* would have been sufficient in preventing the financial crisis. However, the fact remains that the crisis occurred at a time when Glass-Steagall was not no longer in effect, and was but a distant memory. It had been repealed years earlier with Gramm-Leach-Bliley, and along with it disappeared the limitations it had intended to place on banks and financial institutions and protections intended for American investors.

The old saying "when the cat is away, the mice will play" could easily be rewritten to something akin to "when regulations die, bankers will fly." The meaning would remain the same: Lack of proper supervision can have disastrous consequences. The fact remains that for "more than 60 years after it was passed, the Glass-Steagall organization of the commercial banking system ensured that no U.S. bank failure triggered failures or bailouts of other banks" (Ogden, 2015, p. 14). It is difficult to argue with that.

The bankers at Lehman Brothers, AIG, Merrill Lynch, Bear Stearns, and others – while under no supervision – did indeed fly. The flight, with its risky behavior and lack of scruples, was scary for the passengers and ended in a crash landing for the entire U.S. economy. However, as did the mythological phoenix[17], the U.S. economy will slowly rise from the ashes and eventually will be stronger than ever. The U.S may face similar crises in the future. However, if our leaders can find the wisdom to implement provisions contained in the Glass-Steagall Act, events such as the Great Recession and other potential meltdowns can be avoided. Global financial leadership is at stake, and this is a role and an opportunity that should not be squandered.

Glass-Steagall is history, but an import part of history. It kept the United States financially stable throughout many decades. While it may not be possible to re-enact the exact same Glass-Steagall Act that was created long ago, "we should put in place a modern version of Glass-Steagall and separate plain-vanilla banking like checking accounts and savings accounts from crazy risk-taking on Wall Street" (Warren, 2017, p. 93). It could even be modified to address more modern issues. "Since repeal of Glass-Steagall in 1999, after more than a decade of *de facto* inroads, super-banks have been able to re-enact the same kinds of structural conflicts of interest that were endemic in the 1920s" (Engdahl, 2010, p. 316). These conflicts of

---

[17] The phoenix is a Greek mythological bird that supposedly rises from the ashes of its predecessor, thus making a regenerating life form.

interest should be enough for the government to act and create new Glass-Steagall legislation. For "leaving the *status quo* in place is to guarantee another crisis in the future" (Ritholtz, 2009, p. xxii). Now "it's [again] time to return to a banking system divided into two halves: speculative investing and underwriting, and commercial taxpayer-backed depository banks" (*ibid.*, p. xxvi). After all that has transpired, "how could the re-regulation of the banking sector, a deleveraging of capital markets, and meaningful reform of Wall Street not soon become the law of the land" (*ibid.*, p. xxii)?

It is important to understand what caused a problem before a solution can be created. In the case of the Great Recession, the first step is "understanding what led the nation to the brink of financial ruin." (*ibid.*, p. xxii). A new regulatory institution should be created; "bank regulation should be handled by a more suitable regulator" than the Fed (*ibid.*, p. xxvi). Once this has been done, the U.S. government can seek to "bring back competition to the banking sector, [And] limit the size of the behemoths to no more than 5 percent of the total U.S. deposits" (*ibid.*, p. xxvi). Banks no longer considered to be too big to fail would then cease to exist entirely, bringing back financial institutions that can no longer hold the American economy hostage with their short-sighted, high-risk behavior.

Credit default swaps would no longer rise to the popularity they enjoyed in the first decade of the 21st century. Regulation would be reinstated, "eliminating all the useless, worthless debt of the derivatives" (Zepp-LaRouche, 2016, p. 4). After all that has been attained, the next step would be to "go for a global Glass-Steagall separation of the banks in the tradition of Franklin D. Roosevelt" (*ibid.*, p.4). "There is no need to panic over the danger of a 'financial crash'; Glass-Steagall is the solution" (Ingraham, 2015, p. 8). While it is true that, "during the crisis, the Fed did a terrible job of overseeing banking and maintaining basic lending standards" (Ritholtz, 2009, p. xxvi).

However, if a new oversight organization were created – and with the lessons learned – it would hopefully be able to do a better job of monitoring the financial situation. "If Glass-Steagall were still in effect, the banks would have had little incentive to buy the junk from the brokers" (*ibid.*, p. 137).

As is the case in national politics, with each presidential election comes new hope. Hope that the nation's leader will understand the fragility of the economy and the potential catalysts for financial catastrophes. However, hope was dimmed with the election of Donald J. Trump to the U.S. presidency. Already in his first year, deregulation – including financial deregulation – is once again on the table. Among the many promises he has made, one really stands out. Donald Trump "promises to 'unleash' corporations to create more jobs by, among other things, reducing regulations" (Warren, 2017, p. 80). Unfortunately, this will take us back to where we started.

In the present day with globalization, very few crises are limited to a nation's borders. The Great Recession affected not only the United States, but to some degree the entire world. Looking forward, while trying to avoid such crises, it is important to consider that even local measures can have a global impact. Therefore, it is safe to say that "if the United States would take the leadership in going back to Glass-Steagall ... then there would be a platform for the United States to cooperate with the BRIC countries[18] in building the New Silk Road[19]" (Zepp-LaRouche, 2016, p. 5). Additionally, "the anticipated re-enactment of Glass-Steagall legislation in the United States will be the single indispensable action needed to shatter the power of the financial speculators of London and Wall Street" (Ingraham, 2015, p. 7). It would certainly go a long way in helping to "save the trans-Atlantic economic system" (*ibid.*, p. 7). Simply put, "not passing Glass-Steagall now would be fatal for the United States and really for the world" (Ogden, 2015, p. 14). Citizens should call for the "immediate re-instatement of Glass-Steagall, the termination of all of the derivatives contracts on a specific designated date, and the criminal prosecution of all of the TBTF[20] bankers who looted their own customers" (Spannaus, 2016, p. 2).

It is not as if nothing has been done since the crisis. A number of things have changed a little since the Great

---

[18] BRIC countries include Brazil, Russia, India, and China
[19] The New Silk Road is an initiative created by the U.S. to help integrate Central and Southern Asia into international markets.
[20] Too big to fail.

Recession; according to John Cassidy of the New Yorker magazine:
- banks are not as highly leveraged as in 2008
- more criteria have been placed on bonuses and other financial rewards, especially where high risk is involved
- more bonuses are paid in cash or company shares, not stock options
- more scrutiny is paid to the issuance of loans, mortgages, and other financial instruments
- there is more public awareness about the actions of the financial sector.

Yet, there are still banks too big to fail, fewer of them, but behemoths. (Cassidy, 2013, online, accessed 2017-10-11). This fact is very disheartening to many Americans, especially those who lost everything in 2008. For them, it is too little, too late.

As human beings, we strive to learn from our mistakes. This is one thing that separates us from other primates. Yet, we often find ourselves making the same mistake over and over again, each time expecting a different result.

It is imperative that we prevent such a financial disaster from happening again, yet so many important questions remain: Will we really learn from the Great Recession? What can we do to prevent it from happening again? "How should the financial crisis change how we teach economics?" (Mirowski, 2014, p. 67). And most importantly, how do we ensure that our children learn to trust the financial sector again? A new "21st-Century Glass-Steagall Act" (Ogden, 2015, p. 12) would help all citizens, whether in the United States or abroad, learn to trust again.

LIST OF GRAPHS AND TABLES

Graphs

    Graph 1: Common Stock Prices, 1920-1935... ...14
    Graph 2: NASDAQ Composite. 39
    Graph 3: Dow Jones (19-Jul-1987 through 19-Jan-1988). 41
    Graph 4: The Oil Price Record Since 2002 44
    Graph 5: U.S. Subprime Lending Expanded Significantly 2004-2006 55
    Graph 6: Subprime Losses. 58
    Graph 7: Mortgage Delinquencies by Loan Type 60
    Graph 8: Stockmarket Losses During Selected Financial Crises. 74

Tables

    Table 1: Bailout Figures for Major U.S. Automakers 86

BIBLIOGRAPHY

Foreign Sources

CHOSSUDOVSKY, M. and MARSHALL, A. *The Global Economic Crisis*. 1st ed. Montreal, Canada: Global Research, 2010. ISBN 978-1-78168-302-6.

ENGDAHL, F. *Gods of Money*. 1st ed. Wiesbaden, Germany: Joshua Tree, 2010. ISBN 978-3-9813263-1-4.

INGRAHAM, R. The Coming Interim Presidency Under Glass-Steagall: The Name of the Future Is Alexander Hamilton. *Executive Intelligence Review*, 2015, Vol. 42, No. 28, p 7-11. ISSN 0273-6314.

KRUGMAN, P. *The Return of Depression Economics and the Crisis of 2008*. 1st ed. New York: W.W. Norton, 2009. ISBN 978-0-393-33780-8.

MIROWSKI, P. *Never Let a Serious Crisis Go to Waste*. 1st ed. London: Verso, 2014. ISBN 978-1-78168-302-6.

OGDEN, M. Senate Glass-Steagall Move Creates A Potential 'New Era for Mankind'. *Executive Intelligence Review*, 2015, Vol. 42, No. 28, p 12-24. ISSN 0273-6314.

SASS, E., PEARSON, W., and HATTIKUDUR, M. The mental Floss history of the United States: The (almost) complete and (entirely) entertaining story of America. ebook ed. New York: Harper Collins, 2011. ISBN 978-0-06-201434-4.

RITHOLTZ, B. *Bailout nation*. 1st ed. Hoboken, N.J.: Wiley, 2009. ISBN 978-0-470-59632-6.

SPANNAUS, N. Impose Glass-Steagall Now-Before Deutsche Bank Blow-Out. *Executive Intelligence Review*, 2016, Vol. 43, No. 41, p 2. ISSN 0273-6314.

SPEED, D. We Are Entering a New State of the World Economy With the Four Senators' Reintroduction of Glass-Steagall. *Executive Intelligence Review*, 2015, Vol. 42, No. 28, p 54-69. ISSN 0273-6314.

WARREN, E. *This Fight Is Our Fight*. 1st ed. [S.l.]: New York: Macmillan.,2017. ISBN 978-1-250-12061-8.

ZEPP-LAROUCHE, H. Bringing America Into the New Paradigm. *Executive Intelligence Review*, 2016, Vol. 43, No. 41, p 24-30. ISSN 0273-6314.

REFERENCES

AMADEO, K. *What Was the Bank Bailout Bill?* [online]. [cit. 2017-01-06]. Available at: https://www.thebalance.com/what-was-the-bank-bailout-bill-3305675.

AMADEO, K. *Was the big 3 auto bailout worth it?* [online]. [cit. 2017-01-08]. Available at: https://www.thebalance.com/auto-industry-bailout-gm-ford-chrysler-3305670.

BINDER, A. *World's Auto Makers Slammed by Financial Crisis in 2008*. [online]. © 6. 24. 2009 [cit. 2017-09-20]. Available at: http://wardsauto.com/news-analysis/world-s-auto-makers-slammed-financial-crisis-2008.

CARPENTER, D., MURPHY, E., and MURPHY, M. *The Glass-Steagall Act: A Legal and Policy Analysis.* [online] © 1. 19. 2016 [cit. 2017-08-29]. Available at: https://fas.org/sgp/crs/misc/R44349.pdf.

CASSIDY, J. *What Has Changed Since Lehman Failed?* [online]. © 8. 28. 2013 [cit. 2017-10-11]. Available at: https://www.newyorker.com/news/john-cassidy/what-has-changed-since-lehman-failed.

CECCHETTI, S., MANCINI-GRIFFOLI, T., and NARITA, M. *Does Prolonged Monetary Policy Easing Increase Financial Vulnerability?* [online]. © 2. 24. 2017 [cit. 2017-10-11]. Available at: https://www.imf.org/en/Publications/WP/Issues/2017/03/24/Does-Prolonged-Monetary-Policy-Easing-Increase-Financial-Vulnerability-44760.

CLARK, A. *Automotive industry: Carmaker Ford facing dire financial crisis.* [online]. © 6. 20. 2008 [cit. 2017-09-20]. Available at: https://www.theguardian.com/business/2008/jun/20/automotive.useconomy.

COLLINS, M. The big bank bailout. *Forbes.* [online]. © 7. 14. 2015 [cit. 2017-01-06]. Available at: http://www.forbes.com/sites/mikecollins/2015/07/14/the-big-bank-bailout/#71346b903723.

Contribution of the Automotive Industry to the Economies of All Fifty States and the United States. [online]. © 2015 [cit. 2017-09-20]. Available at: http://www.cargroup.org/wp-content/uploads/2017/02/Contribution-of-the-Automotive-Industry-to-the-Economies-of-All-Fifty-States-and-the-United-States2015.pdf.

DURDEN, T. *The Charts From The FCIC Report.* [online]. © 1. 27. 2011 [cit. 2017-10-11]. Available at: http://www.zerohedge.com/article/charts-fcic-report.

EVANS, R. *The biggest stock market crashes in history.* [online] © 9. 9. 2014 [cit. 2017-10-22]. Available at: http://www.telegraph.co.uk/finance/personalfinance/investing/shares/11081763/The-biggest-stock-market-crashes-in-history.html.

Federal Reserve Bank of New York. *The Glass-Steagall Act a.k.a. The Banking Act of 1933.* [online]. [cit. 2017-01-06]. Available at: https://archive.org/details/FullTextTheGlass-steagallActA.k.a.TheBankingActOf1933.

GEIER, B. *What Did We Learn From the Dotcom Stock Bubble of 2000?* [online] © 3. 12. 2015 [cit. 2017-05-03]. Available at: http://time.com/3741681/2000-dotcom-stock-bust/.

HARTLEY, J. *Why Glass-Steagall would not have prevented the financial crisis and could have made it worse.* [online] © 12. 27. 2015 [cit. 2017-01-06]. Available at: http://www.forbes.com/sites/jonhartley/2015/12/27/why-glass-steagall-would-not-have-prevented-the-financial-crisis-and-could-have-made-it-worse/#23cff87a79b7.

KELLEHER, D. The lessons of repealing glass Steagall. *Huffington Post.* [online]. © 11. 11. 2015 [cit. 2017-01-06]. Available at: http://www.huffingtonpost.com/dennis-m-kelleher/the-lessons-of-repealing-glass-steagall_b_8532666.html.

MINTON, B., STULZ, R., and WILLIAMSON, R., 2009, *How much do banks use credit derivatives to hedge loans?* [online]. ©, 2009 [cit. 9. 5. 2017]. Available at: http://www.nber.org/papers/w11579.pdf.

RITHOLTZ, B. *Charts for the "Facts of the Economic Crisis" Column - The Big Picture.* [online]. © 11. 20. 2011 [cit. 2017-10-11]. Available at: http://ritholtz.com/2011/11/charts-facts-economic-crisis/.

SEMUELS, A. *What to Do With a Dying Neighborhood.* [online]. © 1. 14. 2015 [cit. 2017-11-09]. Available at: https://www.theatlantic.com/business/archive/2015/01/what-to-do-with-a-dying-neighborhood/384475/?utm_source=atlfb.

SWAGEL, P. *The impact of the September 2008 economic collapse.* [online]. © 4. 20. 2010 [cit. 2017-01-06] Available at: http://www.pewtrusts.org/en/research-and-analysis/reports/2010/04/28/the-impact-of-the-september-2008-economic-collapse.

TAKIN, M. *Oil-price patterns—1: Oil prices reflect uneven growth rates of global demand and supply*. [online]. © 4. 7. 2014 [cit. 2017-10-11]. Available at: http://www.ogj.com/articles/print/volume-112/issue-4/general-interest/oil-price-patterns-mdash-1-oil-prices-reflect-uneven-growth-rates-of-global-demand-and-supply.html.

ZEESE, K. *The Causes of the Auto Crisis*. [online]. © 11. 24. 2008 [cit. 2017-09-20]. Available at: https://www.counterpunch.org/2008/11/24/the-causes-of-the-auto-crisis/.

ACKNOWLEDGEMENTS

I would like to take this opportunity to thank doc. Ing. Ilona Švihlíková Ph.D, for her guidance, counseling, and patience. I would also like to thank doc. PhDr. JUDr Jakub Rákosník Ph.D. for leading the MBA program at Jan Amos University. Many thanks to Vince McCaffrey, the editor of the book. And, of course, I would like to thank my family for showing patience while I wrote this book.

PUBLICATIONS BY JAMES BRANAM

Mistaken Identity – A Bill Lorentz mystery
Učíme se četbou 1: The Chips Are Down – A Bill Lorentz mystery
Učíme se četbou 2: Mistaken Identity – A Bill Lorentz mystery
Angličtina pro pracovníky v železniční přepravě
English for the Graduation Exam
Učíme se četbou 1 The Chips Are Down (new issue) – A Bill Lorentz mystery
Učíme se četbou 2: Mistaken Identity (new issue) – A Bill Lorentz mystery
Practice in Translation – with Iva Dostálová
Angličtina do dlaně pro střední školy – with Iva Dostálová
Angličtina do dlaně pro základní školy – with Iva Dostálová
Angličtina - Minikoska pro ZŠ – with Iva Dostálová
Angličtina - Minikoska pro SŠ – with Iva Dostálová
Angličtina pro samouky – with Iva Dostálová and Šárka Zelenková
Angličtina pro pro pokročilé samouky – with Iva Dostálová
Angličtina nejen do auta – with Iva Dostálová
Anglicky doma, snadno a rychle – with Iva Dostálová and Šárka Zelenková
WC English (green) – with Iva Dostálová
WC English (red) – with Iva Dostálová
Angličtina - 5 minut denně – with Iva Dostálová
Angličtina -11 minut denně – with Iva Dostálová
Němčina pro samouky – with Barbara Hochheim and Eva Hereinová
Němčina snadno a rychle – with Barbara Hochheim and Eva Hereinová
Angličtina pre samoukov– with Iva Dostálová and Šárka Zelenková (Slovak)
Angličtina pre pokročilých samoukov – with Iva Dostálová (Slovak)
Anglų Kalba Savarankiškai – with Iva Dostálová and Šárka Zelenková (Lithuanian)
Anglu Valodas Pašmácíba – with Iva Dostálová and Šárka Zelenková (Latvian)
Anglu Valodas Pašmácíba 2– with Iva Dostálová and Šárka Zelenková (Latvian)
Angielski dla samouków– with Iva Dostálová and Šárka Zelenková (Polish)
Nemčina pre samoukov – with Barbara Hochheim and Eva Hereinová (Slovak)
Easy English with Beautiful Music (Volume 1) – with Pavel Rynt
Easy English with Beautiful Music (Volume 2) – with Pavel Rynt
Easy English with Beautiful Music (Volume 3) – with Pavel Rynt
Easy English with Beautiful Music (Volume 4) – with Pavel Rynt
The Easy Way Out, a novel

AUTHOR BIOGRAPHY

James Michael Branam was born in Seymour, Indiana. After finishing high school, during which he studied Russian, German, French, and Spanish, he spent six years in the U.S. Air Force as a Czech and Slovak linguist. He was sent to West Germany during the Cold War. In 1993, he moved to the Czech Republic where he taught high school for nearly ten years (English and German). In 2002, he moved to the United Stated to return to college where he received a B.A. in English and a B.A. in German from Oregon State University, both summa cum laude. He received is M.B.A. from Jan Amos Komenský University in Prague in 2018.

Today, he is the author of more than 30 language textbooks that have been published in seven countries. Although this is his first novel, he has written many short stories, a few of which have been publish in periodicals.

www.ingramcontent.com/pod-product-compliance
Lightning Source LLC
Chambersburg PA
CBHW070319220526
45465CB00013B/1316